COVENANT POWER

TRANSFORM FEAR INTO FAITH
THROUGH THE POWER OF JESUS CHRIST

SHARLA GOETTL

COVENANT POWER

TRANSFORM FEAR INTO FAITH THROUGH THE POWER OF JESUS CHRIST

CFI
An imprint of Cedar Fort, Inc.
Springville, Utah

Paperback ISBN 13: 978-1-4621-5048-9
eBook ISBN 13: 978-1-4621-5049-6

Published by CFI, an imprint of Cedar Fort, Inc.
2373 W. 700 S., Suite 100, Springville, UT 84663
Distributed by Cedar Fort, Inc., www.cedarfort.com

Library of Congress Cataloging Number:

Cover design by Shawnda Craig
Cover design © 2026 Cedar Fort, Inc.
Edited by Jessica Lawrence
Typeset by Liz Kazandzhy

Printed in the United States of America

10 9 8 7 6 5 4 3 2 1

Printed on acid-free paper

To my eternal family.

We'll be in the temple together one day.

Contents

Introduction

LET'S IMAGINE FOR A MINUTE WHAT THE PERFECT UNIVERSITY WOULD be like.

Everyone would be known and valued. The tuition would be set on a sliding scale perfectly matched to your ability to pay, with a very generous grace agreement. You wouldn't have to go through the dreaded process of picking a major, because you would be so well understood that your degree would perfectly fit your full potential, preparing you for what you will find most invigorating and fulfilling. The teaching style would be personalized to how you retain information best. The lesson plans would include only eternal truth and wisdom.

Further, the value of this education would be unquestioned—its skills would be universally applicable and nowhere else to be found. The school would have a long-proven record of its students accepting the most impactful job offers imaginable. The alumni association would be particularly influential and supportive. The dean would never once compromise your best interest, and your fellow students would make it their mission to help you along your educational journey. As a bonus, palace-like campuses would be springing up in cities all over the world.

Sounds great, right? Miraculously, it's already available! This is a description of God's university—the temple of God, the house of the Lord. Here you will learn more about Heavenly Father's plan for your happiness. It is here that you will learn the skills Jesus Christ mastered. With time in the temple and practice at home, you will be prepared for Him to share His power with you.

How Do You Start?

Covenant principles are valuable and sacred because they lead you to power. Taught within the house of the Lord, they help you cut through the noise and distraction to focus on what creates God-like success. The covenants made in the temple—the laws of the gospel, obedience, sacrifice, chastity, and consecration—are the greatest skills I know. They have been authored by God, taught by Christ, and confirmed by the Holy Ghost. These skills will never be proven irrelevant or insufficient. Presented as two-way promises with Heavenly Father, these endowment covenants make me less fearful and help me see clearly how to get what I want most.

The temple is a solidly built sanctuary of truths where you can feel confident and safe. Think of the temple walls as tangible evidence of Heavenly Father's love. Inside, there is no misdirection from unproven theories, shallow arrogance, or false promises—only clear strategies for success. Inside, Christ is trying to lead you along your covenant path toward getting what you want in the most long-lasting way.

Holiness to the Lord is a fitting description of the revelatory experiences that occur at the individual level within the temple. These revelations bring us closer to Him. While the milestones of the covenant path are the same for all of God's children, you walk a path with different questions and experiences than I do. In the temple, you will have greater access to the Holy Ghost. You can hear answers and directions spoken just to you. In this way, your covenant path takes on a unique shape.

Similarly, all of us were born with the potential to live celestially. But we are not all fulfilled in the same way or excited about the same things. Yet Heavenly Father's promises are made one by one within the temple, ensuring that what our Father wants for you truly includes what you want for yourself. It is not His work to betray you with anything less than your eternal joy. Christ will help you every time you act in a short-sighted way, and Heavenly Father will always respect your agency. Accepting that God understands what will make you happiest is always your choice, but it is an important step in your learning process.

Two things happen when you initiate a strong bond of partnership with Heavenly Father. With permission, you approach Him and with permission, He will approach you. Jesus Christ enables both steps.

1. Demonstrate your understanding of the doctrine of Jesus Christ by worthily receiving a temple recommend (Christ's authorization).
2. Demonstrate your desire to receive His partnership by participating in temple ordinances (your authorization).

Just as a contract requires a signature, a covenant partnership requires proof of your understanding and freely given acceptance. These two steps represent two signatures on a divinely valid contract.

My friend, as you live in this partnership, remove those habits that you know are holding you back. Don't make life harder than it needs to be. Your interaction with God will make all the difference in your current choices and future success. Seek Heavenly Father's more effective solutions to your obstacles. Talk to Him about your questions regularly. He will answer your fears about the future with hope and confidence. Temple covenants and Christ's grace will enable you to progress beyond what you can do alone. I shall do my best to explain *how* this is true.

Our Saving Ordinances

Before we talk about temple covenants, I want to briefly emphasize the sacred significance of the five covenant principles within the endowment (obedience, sacrifice, the gospel of Christ, chastity, and consecration). They are not just guidelines for mortals; they are eternal principles—even effective tools of divinity. Elohim learned them and used them to enact the plan of salvation. Jehovah learned them and used them to become our Savior. The Holy Ghost learned them and will always testify to their power. The scriptures illustrate Christ teaching these principles, from the Garden of Eden through the Restoration. They act as a user's manual to the principles that will prepare us to live and work with God one day.

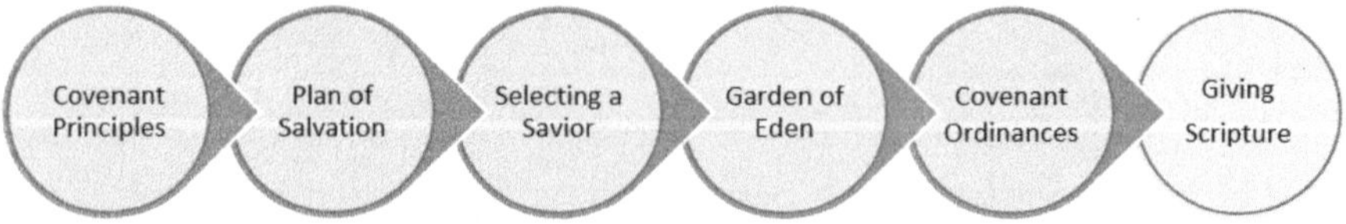

Think about how covenant principles are the bedrock elements in each step of the plan of salvation, including mortality, the Atonement, redemption, the Resurrection, and exaltation. Covenant principles came first. Without them, "the whole earth would be utterly wasted at his coming" (Joseph Smith—History 1:39).

God emphasizes the importance of these covenant principles by presenting them to you as covenant ordinances within His temple. By accepting and consistently living these covenants while relying on the grace of Jesus Christ, you are activating priesthood power to change you into who you need to be for exaltation.

Hold these covenant principles in priority as you strive for progress through Jesus Christ. He does not ask this of you to force subordination. He asks this of you to further your exaltation. Covenant principles lead to godly priesthood power. Jesus Christ is our proof that they work as promised.

The Narratives

Throughout the endowment ordinance, a visual presentation teaches you about each phase of the plan of salvation. In the video, you will hear Heavenly Father instructing Jesus Christ and the archangel Michael in creating the earth. You will also observe Adam and Eve in the Garden of Eden as they receive covenants. This visual is powerful because seeing Adam and Eve from a first-person point of view has given me deeper insight into their intentions, character, and learning process. I have gained more understanding of *why* and *how* they made their heroic choices.

This book will follow a similar teaching strategy to the temple video. I will highlight scriptural stories that demonstrate the power of each covenant principle. These first-person narratives are based on the words and experiences of scriptural heroes who taught and lived each of the endowment covenant principles, but from an imaginary perspective. For example:

- Jacob, as a patriarch, teaches about the overarching new and everlasting covenant.
- Michael and Eve, as new learners, teach about the Creation.
- Nephi, as a teenager, demonstrates the law of obedience.
- Sariah, as a mother, teaches the law of sacrifice.
- Corianton, through his repentance, teaches the law of the gospel of Jesus Christ.
- Mormon, as a young adult, teaches the law of chastity.
- Nephi III, a prophet, teaches the law of consecration.

Scriptural stories offer true, living examples of how our Savior empowers capable leaders, teachers, and children of God who honor their covenants. We know each of these people became much more than they ever thought possible because they lived their covenants. These Saints are testifying that temple covenants work! Their words were miraculously preserved to enrich and expand your understanding of the covenant path in these latter days.

I hope that by adding context to these true accounts, you can understand *why* and *how* these people kept their covenants. Following each narrative, I will provide commentary that further explains the covenant principle.

Revelatory Disclaimer

Importantly, I want to note that my narratives are simply *possibilities* of how these individuals' stories could have played out—nothing more. These narratives are not a strict retelling of scriptural accounts. Instead, I have used creative license to highlight covenant-keeping within the life of someone you already know and respect. Hopefully, this will help you to imagine *yourself* as the covenant keeper within these stories more fully.

I encourage you to revise my versions and to seek out more stories within the scriptures where these covenant principles are taught. For me, it has sparked profound insights from the Holy Ghost.

My goal is to build a bridge between your study of the scriptures, the temple covenants taught in the endowment, and your own lived experiences. Every page of scripture was written to teach us about

Christ. He came to empower our covenant relationship with Heavenly Father. So there are so many more connections to be found.

As you will hear in the temple, the endowment is best understood through revelation. This book can spark questions that lead to revelatory spiritual insights. I was hesitant to write this book, so as not to impose on the temple learning experience, but the Spirit consistently prompted me to complete it. I honor the refining input of the Holy Ghost in this work and claim any misperceptions as mine alone.

Chapter 1

The Abrahamic Covenant

Jacob

To be known as Israel or "Let God Prevail"
Father of the Twelve Tribes
Along the River Jabbok
See Genesis 27–32

I HAVE OFTEN GAZED UPON THE INNUMERABLE STARS SHINING ABOVE my head. God has prophesied that those stars are mine—every single one of them. Those stars in their glory represent my glorious future children. Ever since, those stars have been as overwhelming to me as they have been beautiful to behold. My whole life, their brightness has entreated me, goaded me, even intimidated me. I have wanted to touch them, but also feared that I might cause their fall.

God has spoken. One day, I will know them and love them. I will speak counsel, and they will hear me. They will sing praises to God, and I will hear them. God has promised that I will be a patriarch of His covenantal family, which will expand to an uncountable number. Each member of my posterity will hold the potential for glory—even to exceed the stars.

But how is this to be done and by what power? This question has often occupied my thoughts and filled my prayers. If I can't even imagine how it is to be done, then how can *I* be the means whereby it's fulfilled?

My father, Isaac of Moriah, has been sanctified by our God since he was a young man (see Genesis 22). God's touch of salvation has made him wise, stalwart, and kind. He is a fitting symbol of God's sacrificial Lamb. Isaac brought me before the mantle of priesthood power—at the feet of my patriarchal grandfather Abraham—and confirmed all the promises and blessings of which I was taught.

My father and grandfather should have been nothing more than two obscure men of the dusty fields. Caring for livestock should have been their life's purpose. But because of their covenants with God, they have seen visions of the Christ, heard angels, and felt the undeniable burning of the Holy Ghost. They have achieved so much but still do not have all they dream of.

Each has only one covenantal son to share their divine inheritance. How then are their impossibly grand prophesies to be fulfilled? They will be fulfilled with posterity to number the stars, access to redemption across generations, fortune beyond our understanding, fame that will spread across the whole world, and authorization to access the Almighty's priesthood power unto godly exaltation.

Isaac and Abraham waited with such hopeful patience for the Lord's plan. I have asked them how they have the stamina to do so, but I have never understood the optimism in their answers. Why? How? Their answers never satisfied me because I couldn't understand the weight and strength of God's power. I didn't possess enough context to see how far God's power could reach. I did not yet know enough to be reassured.

But now I do. Now I know for myself what my ancestors have known for a long time. It's as if I once held pebbles of knowledge, but now I stand on a mountain of truth. Tonight's experience with the Lord has given me a higher perspective, from which I can now see more clearly into His plan. I now stand on firmer ground, which grants me a clearer understanding of the work God has called me to.

As I look at the stars now, with God's vision my own, I am seeing them anew for the first time.

I wish to tell you my story. I need you to see how God has led my path of salvation from my early days, preparing me for a work I must accomplish.

It started many, many years ago. As a child, hearing the teachings of my forebearers always filled me with wonder and peace. God was good. God was intelligence. God was there for me. But my twin brother Esau felt quite differently. We learned the same lessons and heard the same stories, but while I saw strength, he saw weakness.

God had taught my grandfather the mysteries of heaven, but Esau considered Abraham's studies to be a distraction from what was real. God had saved my father on the sacrificial altar, but Esau saw Isaac's willingness to submit as a vulnerability. To be at the mercy of anyone or anything was intolerable to Esau. He thought that depending on another, even God, diminished him. Any outcome was better than showing weakness or being trapped by another's expectations.

Esau grew to be brawny and bold but obsessively focused on avoiding a state of vulnerability. He spent his time on whatever would make him stronger, more skilled, or more influential. He carelessly traded his birthright to me to prove he didn't really need it—his future was in his own hands. He married women of Canaan to prove that no limitation applied to him—he could marry whoever he wanted.

However, there were times when his arrogance faltered, and his true feelings came to the surface. Esau could not hide his disappointment when our father unknowingly conferred the priesthood upon me instead of him. The momentary sign of inferiority made him intensely angry. His anger was focused on me, not because he wanted the responsibility of the priesthood, but because I made him appear weak, for he had lost something of immense value. My blessing sparked a feeling of shame in my brother. Deep in his heart, he knew the inheritance was bestowed correctly and that he had not lived worthy of his birthright. If I were eliminated, he thought his shame could die with me, and the inheritance would once again be his.

The twin brother of my birth called for my death. I had to run away at the urgent pleading of my parents. But I did not deny God in my distress. I could not deny that I hoped for Him and His promises.

So instead, I ran from my home, my family, and my land. My faith in God's promises was still intact. I headed toward the distant home of my uncle Laban with the hope that at some future time, it would be safe enough to return.

Unfortunately, my relief was only temporary. Walking to Haran from Beersheba was its own kind of death sentence. Four hundred fifty miles across harsh, unfamiliar wilderness included months of exposure and deprivation for an unprepared, lone man. I wasn't young, but I had never been this exposed before. I was so afraid of this new vulnerability—destitute for the first time, forced to beg for protection, stripped of all control over my life. Did Adam feel this way walking away from the Garden of Eden? At least he wasn't alone.

Not more than a few days' journey north toward Haran, I lay down to sleep with nothing but a stone as my pillow. That evening, God visited me in a vivid dream (see Genesis 28:10–22).

Above me in the air, the dark azure skies opened to reveal a world otherwise unseen but as real as the one in which I live. Stretching from the ground to the star-dazzling heavens appeared a ladder—or stairway—of several steps. Sturdy, unwavering, and glowing as an everlasting flame, these steps were reliable and constant. Upon them moved angels—men and women of God. With evident purity and power, these sentinels moved freely up and down the steps.

My mind perceived more than my eyes could see. I could sense their power as subjects of God. I could feel their purpose and satisfaction. This vision sparked many new questions, but I also recognized with clarity that I lacked what they had. They had protection that would never be taken from them. They had the capability to control their outcome. I began to realize that becoming like them may be part of how I fulfill my duty so God's grand promises could come true.

The stairs started right where I was. It wouldn't take more than a few strides before reaching the first step. As I gazed upward along the solid steps, I realized they led to where I wanted to be. I wanted to be among those stars—among my future-glorified, worldwide family. Suddenly, I understood the magnificent lesson that the Messiah was so beautifully illustrating for me—that the covenant path was available, accessible, and within my capacity to climb. I only needed to take one step at a time. His steps of salvation stretched so much further than I had imagined they could.

Understanding that God had endowed me with a sacred gift, I dedicated the place in which I had camped and seen this vision. Calling the place Bethel, or "the house of God," I built and anointed an altar in this sacred space to mark the lifelong promise I made to Him. If He returned me safely back to my home, I would serve Him all my days.

Having survived my long journey, I first laid eyes on my future wife several weeks later on the outskirts of Haran. I still hold pieces of memory from that day. Her long auburn hair was the finest thing I had seen in months. It shone in the setting sunlight as she walked along the dirt road. She held a blue scarf but dropped it, then snatched it up just before her sheep could step on it. I remember watching her laugh at herself before she even noticed I was there.

She was so beautiful to my dreary eyes. There was a light emanating from her that I had never perceived in any other woman. It was only by the hand of God that the future keeper of my heart—my dear Rachel— would have come to the same well as I.

The years that followed flew by with hard work and quick progress. God never failed in His promises to me, always turning a difficult situation to my advantage.

When my father-in-law thought of cheating me into marrying his eldest daughter, Leah, little did he know how much I would need her. May God be praised for knowing what I needed even more than I did myself. As the blessed matron of our large family, Leah has given me wise counsel and steadfast partnership that has been my solace through many days.

Though I have withstood many trials, my hardships have been well borne. My wealth and family have grown despite circumstances that would have easily hindered other men, thanks to the strength the Lord has given me. I am now the father of a great many sons and daughters, with four wives who depend on me and care for me.

It was one year ago that a burning in my heart could no longer be dismissed. God was directing me to return home, back to Beersheba. Rachel finally had a child of her own, our dear little one, Joseph. With her emotional weight graciously lifted at last, the time to leave her home and return to my own finally felt right.

I have no reason to believe Esau's anger has calmed over the years. What's more, he has grown even more influential over time. In the twenty years since my escape from Beersheba, God has kept His promises to Esau as well (see Genesis 27:39–41). He has become a man of great reputation and authority. While I have built up a great multitude of sheep and children, he has built up an army of men. At his command, my family could be slaughtered, my household enslaved, and my flocks stolen. My entire life would become forfeit.

With each southward mile, my dread would not be calmed. I sent ahead scouts who reported back all I had feared. Esau approached with no less than 400 men. I was racked with guilt for putting my family in such danger and desperately considered every option.

Seven days ago, I chose a wooded spot along the banks of the River Jabbok to camp, water the herds, and consider my next move. I arranged for large waves of gifts to be sent ahead in Esau's name. Perhaps 600 animals would be enough to encumber his forces.

In truth, I feel no pity at the loss of my herds. It felt right to give them to him. After all, I did indeed desire his birthright for myself, and I treasure it still today. And despite all the circumstances, I knew in my heart it would hurt him. If I can in any way make amends by offering him the bounty God has given me, I hope to do so.

Over the last few days, my wives and children could read the distress across my brow, filling their hearts with fear. It was my responsibility to protect them. I chose to bring them into this danger, far from the comfortable tents and fires of Haran. How am I any different from Abraham, who hiked up a mountain intent on sacrificing his one son? I have knowingly placed all eleven of my sons in mortal danger, along with the whole of my household!

Yesterday, I placed my family far from me on the other side of the river, pitifully hoping that perhaps it would act as a barrier if Esau attacked in the night. With all possible preparations complete, I waited alone as the camp across the water settled down to sleep. The firelight of the sentries reflected off the water. The breeze was crisp and cool. I strained to hear if it brought the sound of galloping horses, but the night was silent and all was calm.

The sky darkened, and the stars began to shine above my head once more. The stars were completely unconcerned that the dangerous dawn could bring my complete and utter destruction. As I lay on my back in the cold grass, sleep was far from me. I stared at those stars that felt so far away. Were they disappointed that I found myself in such a precarious situation? Pressure mounted in my heart, and I could barely stand looking at them any longer. I squeezed my eyes shut and desperately pleaded for God's help (see Genesis 32:24–32).

For hours, my mind tumbled from one fear to the next as they multiplied at an overwhelming pace. I was praying to God so long that I felt as though I could envision Him standing before me, listening to my concerns. Yet I allowed no relief to enter my heart. I wanted an explanation more than I wanted peace. My emotions began coming forcefully, even chaotically, shifting quickly between dread, frustration, and logic. Anxious energy filled my limbs, and I stood to pace in agitation. Every heaven-sent plea felt like a grasp at thin air. Eventually, my fear of Esau warped into resentment toward God. Reaching a breaking point, I even threw a blow at the night sky, but it didn't end in empty space. I hit what felt like … flesh.

What had just happened? Was I awake or dreaming?

But there he was, standing directly in front of me. Just what I wanted and just what I needed—a godly man willing to fight it out. Who was this stranger in the dark? I looked at him, but I felt he could look *into* me. He knew how vulnerable I was, and I knew he could do something about it. Could I make him help me?

He squared his shoulders and lowered his head, as if he had heard my thoughts. Irrationally, full of anger and desperation, the fight within me broke its bounds, and I full-on charged the man. He was ready. He countered with a satisfying force to fairly match the fire within me.

All night we thrashed; all night I wrestled with this unknown man of flesh and bone. If I could just hold on to him, he would have to help me. If I could pin him down, he would have to answer my questions. My pride would not allow me to stop. Perhaps I'm more like Esau than I thought. I was fighting to know if I held the power to rescue my family. I needed to know if this man could be beaten.

With one attack after another, I exhausted my immediate worries. As the night dragged on, I dug deeper, tapping into what felt like an unending supply of spiritual troubles and doubts, fueling my fire to physically fight back. I didn't know who he was yet, but the fight in my heart was with God. In my mind, I yelled question after question toward God:

"I can't save them by myself! I can't even protect my children!"

"I don't know what's coming. I don't know what I'm supposed to do!"

"Will you leave me? Or will you fight this fight for me?"

"I'm unprotected in an open plain. Where is the protection I was promised?"

"How can you let me utterly fail like this?"

"Why won't you answer me?"

"Why have you chosen me?"

"Haven't I done what you wanted? Haven't I tried?"

"What more do you want from me? I'm not good enough to do what you want."

"How can I possibly lead the children of men to the Messiah? Why is this my responsibility?"

"I want to be with you. I've done what you asked. But now I'm terrified!"

"Why have you done this to me? Why have you brought me here?"

I needed to fight, and he knew it. I needed a wrestle of the heart, mind, and body. He bore all I could throw at him and let it keep coming. Every time I punched out my fears, he swerved deftly. Every time I attempted to take him down, I faltered against an unmovable weight. Every time I had him trapped, he knew the perfect escape.

When he hit me, his blows resonated deeply, bringing clarity and revelation. When he held back my arms, I knew there was nothing stronger in the world. When he pinned me down, I struggled hard, but he released me only at his choosing. He never once faltered. I found only relentless superiority.

When he flipped me over his back or threw me to the ground, I glimpsed the stars again and again. I'd close my eyes and drag myself up, just to be flipped again moments later.

"Those are your stars," he kept saying in my mind. "I know what I am doing!"

By the time the sun began to rise, my body was bruised and broken, but my mind was clear and active. I realized I no longer needed to be the savior of my family—not my family now, and not the family I was destined to care for. God could save us. God *would* save us! I just had to trust Him. I just had to follow Him.

Proving that he was stronger than me, the man gently touched my hip with one finger. My pelvis broke immediately. I fell to the ground in utter shock and indescribable pain! Unable to lift my own body, I now knew he had power over me and all heaven and earth.

But just as quickly, he healed me. The searing pain was momentary, the healing comfort tangible. Miraculously, he was the source of this healing. But how could this be done? Which is easier, to break a bone or to heal one? (see Matthew 9:1–8)

With my own eyes, I saw he was real. With my own body, I learned of his superior strength and endurance. With my own pain, I felt the contrast of his healing power. His firm resolve and solid strength calmed my questions. I now trusted that he was powerful enough for me.

Exhausted in the early dawn, my body dripping with sweat and dew, I knelt in the dirt and honored the victor.

He asked me to declare my name, which I did willingly.

Then he declared a new name upon me—Israel, which means "let God prevail." [1]

I wondered why he gifted me with a name of power when I had lost the wrestle? But God's wisdom came into my mind. The name was to testify to the *true* source of my power.

This is a name I will repeat for the rest of my life, reminding me of the skill I truly need to develop. Whenever a loved one calls out to me for help, this name will guide them. Whenever future generations pray for home, this name will comfort them. Whenever a covenantal son or daughter needs added strength, this name will remind them to Whom they belong.

Israel, Israel, Israel.

I relented to this man who had fought me throughout the night, distilling comfort and wisdom in unexpected ways. He had certainly prevailed over me.

But who was this man? Could Jehovah Himself be here with me in the flesh? Or could this heavenly fighter instead be Enoch of old or the great Melchizedek, translated beings sent to me by God's grace?

"Tell me, I pray thee, thy name," I asked.

"Wherefore is it that thou dost ask after my name?" He replied. "Do you not know who I am?"

Then, before my eyes, I saw the Man for who He was—the only One who could grant me a covenant of power. This stranger of my troubled night shone with a majesty that made the coming sun look plain and small. Before me stood Elohim, Father of all Heaven, come so far down to answer my questions and instill confidence within my heart.

I saw Him face-to-face.

I embraced the Father of Adam, Enoch, and Noah, even the God of Abraham and Isaac. I released my doubts into those outstretched arms and confidently embraced my new identity to let God prevail forever in my life. I tearfully worshipped Him for helping me overcome the fears of my present battles and my future tasks. I solemnly dedicated my full loyalty to Him.

Once again alone, lying exhausted in the grass, my arms and hands could still feel the warm afterglow of that embrace. My body was spent, and my mind was flooded with insights from my new perspective.

The morning finally broke, and the dawn fully arrived. The sun threw a blanket of warm light over my stars and painted the sky with vivid color. I listened to the birds sing their worshipful songs along the riverbank. The water flowed—ceaseless and steady—the way God's will continued to flow onward. A breeze cooled my heated skin as it filled my lungs with new life.

I will see my brother today. The thought no longer makes me afraid. Esau has no power to change what God wishes to take place. He has laid the steps of my covenant promises before me. I will climb every step of the ladder, for I know God will always prevail.[2]

Endowed with Partnership

Creating an endowed partnership with God in His holy temple is a necessary step toward soul-saving.

Jacob would agree. As he yielded to God, the highest of privileges were sealed upon him: all the blessings promised to his fathers and the ability to enjoy God's presence. Essentially, God's endowment was sealed upon him. As Genesis 32:28–30 states, "Thy name shall be called no more Jacob, but Israel: for as a prince hast thou power with God and with men, and hast prevailed. … And [God] blessed him there. And Jacob called the name of the place Peniel [meaning the face of God]: for I have seen God face-to-face, and my life is preserved."

Your endowment will also bring *you* these incredible benefits. Your endowment can create a deep sense of confidence. But do you understand why this is true? Do you know what promises you make in the temple and what promises are made to you in return? As you look for covenant principles throughout the scriptures, you will see God showing you examples of how revealed covenant ordinances can benefit your life.

The words "fear not" and "glad tidings" take on deeper significance during the endowment because Christ addresses our mortal fears with each covenant, layer by layer, while also promising us our deepest desires one by one. Through consistent righteousness and divine decree, you do not need to be afraid, nor do you need to doubt your ultimate success. This was Heavenly Father's message to Jacob as they wrestled that night. This is the empowering truth found in temples today.

Jacob was very afraid that night. He was afraid of failure in the face of meeting Esau, but he was also afraid of not fulfilling his purpose. We all have fears and doubts about reaching our fullest potential. Jacob's covenantal interactions with God made him confident and hopeful—but they also made him capable. God's covenants gave him the reassurance he needed to know his fears could not hinder his promised successes.

Covenants are how you overcome all that makes you afraid. They are also how you get what you want because God is teaching you His strategies for success. Covenants can brace you when you feel vulnerable and can provide a solid foundation for our growth. Each covenant has a purpose. They interlock seamlessly to create the only sure and safe foundation Christ has promised you (Jacob 4:15–16). In the following chapters, I will explain how each covenant serves to build you up.

The New and Everlasting Covenant

Did you know that God builds temples so He can be accessible to you, just as He was with Abraham, Isaac, and Jacob? The Abrahamic covenant of old is a significant part of the new and everlasting covenant today. They are essentially the same because the old fits within the new. The new and everlasting covenant includes everything Christ has taught or promised. It is now fully and perpetually accessible because temple ordinances were restored.

The key difference between the old covenant and the new covenant is that the old is fulfilled by the new, just as the doctrine of Christ fulfilled the law of Moses. For God to connect Jacob with a posterity as numerous as the stars of the sky, the new and everlasting covenant had to be extended to all of us. "New" refers to all Christ's teachings being renewed. "Everlasting" refers to Christ's covenants being eternally relevant and necessary. The same covenants and doctrines of Christ were essential for all ancient prophets and Saints—including Adam, Enoch, Moses, Abraham, Peter, and Joseph Smith. They are also necessary for all of us. No one can be saved without them.

It's important to understand that every promise, expectation, and hope you have learned from Christ is part of the new and everlasting covenant. All of Christ's promises depend on following commandments and keeping covenants. As His sheep, we cannot continually follow the Shepherd without eventually passing through His covenants. The meek cannot inherit the earth without covenants. The weary cannot perpetually feel peace without covenants.

For thousands of years, Christ has been repeating His plea: "Come unto me." He says it over and over. Where do you think He is? One answer is found in the words of our prophet, President Russell M. Nelson: "Here is my promise to you: Every sincere seeker of Jesus Christ will find Him in the temple." Step by step, Christ has been preparing for temples to be available and for covenants to be authorized again through His priesthood.

Following Jesus's example will make anyone happier. But when Christ teaches us about Himself, it's only in preparation for His true goal, which is to lead us to Heavenly Father! The Holy Ghost and

Jesus Christ welcome you into every temple. Inside, They symbolically introduce you to Heavenly Father.

Every temple is declared the house of the *Lord*, but because you are a child of God—a child of His covenants—the temple is *your* sacred home too. Temples stand on firm foundations set apart from the world, dedicated as your palace of refuge and gateway to joy. Every time you enter, let His hope for you stand out.

Covenants are your golden ticket to the plan of salvation. Faith, repentance, baptism, and receiving the gift of the Holy Ghost are the first steps toward God. But there is so much more God wants for you. The temple endowment lets you climb higher up the covenantal ladder that Jacob saw in his vision. This book will help you understand how, but first you must understand that the ladder is available to you, not just Jacob. It is also within your reach.

As you serve God all your days, temple covenants will reassure you that God will indeed bring you safely home—just like He did for Jacob. By granting you a firm foundation right now and ever-higher opportunities later, these covenants will make your life less fearful and more hopeful, purposeful, and satisfying. With enduring kindness, Heavenly Father wants every willing soul to embrace the promises made in temples throughout the world.

I know from personal experience that your ability to live confidently, love deeply, and work effectively will increase as you better understand temple covenants. You can feel a decrease in fear, loneliness, inadequacy, and vulnerability. The strongest effects of desperation no longer need to apply to you. You can more easily accept that God has declared your eternal success, regardless of your trials. You can more resolutely follow His direction toward reaching that success. It is my testimony that the more you know about temple blessings, the more secure, loved, and excited you will feel about your exhilarating future.

The temple is the only place you can make a promise with the One who has the power to keep that promise perfectly while never compromising your best interests. *You* might at times compromise your long-term joy for short-term happiness, but Heavenly Father never will. Because He is a faithful covenant keeper, Heavenly Father's promises will always be guaranteed. "For the mountains shall depart and the hills be removed, but my kindness shall not depart from thee, neither shall the covenant of my peace be removed, saith the Lord that hath mercy on thee" (3 Nephi 22:10).

Access to Power

Why did your heavenly parents care to send you to earth? Why did Christ sacrifice Himself for your sins? Why did the Holy Ghost dedicate His existence to help you? They have endeavored tremendous work on your behalf. But why do They do it, and what is their end goal?

Their greatest desire is to share their power with you so that you can, in turn, help others receive their needed ordinances (see Doctrine and Covenants 84:20–21). They help you out of love—a love that can't be lost, earned, or even deserved—because they know that once you have learned to be responsible with incredible power, you will use it to do incredible good.

The endowment ordinance is a necessary step in this power-sharing process. As you keep your promises, you improve your character and become more worthy of receiving and using God's power responsibly (see Doctrine and Covenants 121:36–37). As you better understand the promises Heavenly Father makes in return, you can feel a solid sense of security that will increase your motivation to share this opportunity with others.

Perhaps it's difficult to envision God as your Father because He is immortal and glorified. Perhaps it's difficult to imagine Christ as your brother because He was half-immortal and glorified. However, Abraham, Isaac, and Jacob, as well as their wives, were once fully mortal but are *now* immortal and glorified (see Doctrine and Covenants 132:19–20, 28–33). They were born no differently than you and me. They are proof that God's covenantal staircase works as promised, for they have already been endowed, refined, redeemed, judged, resurrected, empowered, and glorified: "Because [Abraham, Isaac, and Jacob] did none other things than that which they were commanded, they have entered into their exaltation, *according to the promises*, and sit upon thrones, and are not angels but are gods" (see Doctrine and Covenants 132:37; emphasis added). Jacob made it to the top of the covenant ladder.

God's covenantal ladder is your inheritance as a literal or adopted member of the house of Israel. You can climb Jacob's ladder just as he did. Jacob let God prevail, becoming a mortal example of divine success for all the house of Israel. Choosing not to receive your endowment is like selling your divine inheritance for a bowl of pottage, as Esau did (see Genesis 25:29–34).[3] The choice is ultimately yours.

What Do You Want Most?

Which promises of God are you most excited about? As you "think celestial" as President Russell M. Nelson (1924–2025) has asked, what part of exaltation are you looking forward to the most? What are the deepest desires of your heart? Why do you want exaltation so much?

The answers are different for everyone, but articulating what you want most will increase your motivation to remain close to Jesus Christ. Only then can you start to understand how Christ is the only source of your true joy. Finding your most sincere answer to these questions will help you better understand why Christ is asking you to be steadfast. He wants you to receive all He has, including what will bring you divine joy.

More than anything else, Jacob wanted to fulfill his responsibilities to his covenantal family. Indeed, we know through modern revelation that he has succeeded in doing so because he kept his covenants. Temple covenants are how you get what you ultimately want, in an eternal way.

I heard a temple president once say that more than anything else, he wanted to be there to welcome his children into their celestial glory. I listened to a mission leader say that her greatest wish was to have the stamina never to stop serving those she loves. I'm so eager to remember the valiant woman I was in my premortal life. Others may want the knowledge of God, lasting peace, or the power to exercise greater control over their lives. Jesus Christ can enable these blessings as we become covenant keepers.

Every time we honor our covenants, we take a micro-step closer to getting what we want. My celestial hopes are realistic, and so are yours—accessible forever in the temple of God. Your heavenly parents know you well. They know the desires of your heart—whether it be marriage, health, friendships, and so on—and are trying to help you as part of your personalized exaltation. "For behold, this is [God's] work and [His] glory—to bring to pass the immortality and eternal life of man" (Moses 1:39).

I'm sure you know this already, but God is incredibly powerful. He is whole, unbroken, and complete. He is so powerful that, simply by learning about Him, your broken parts can begin to heal, making you a little more whole. Partnering with Heavenly Father through covenants speeds up this learning process—not just through influence but through transformation. Covenants grant God your permission and access to change your heart. Being made whole—meaning to become like Christ—involves sharing in God's divine attributes of power. The process will not be complete until after this mortal life, but the process can start now.

Consider the table below. Which Christlike attributes are you most excited about?

Love	Respect	Influence	Security	Family	Peace
Purpose	Patience	Humility	Foresight	Satisfaction	Comfort
Authority	Confidence	Discernment	Bravery	Endurance	Strength
Friendship	Wisdom	Forgiveness	Resilience	Prophecy	Pleasure
Ability	Prosperity	Empathy	Excitement	Freedom	Genius
Creativity	Leadership	Diligence	Authenticity	Charity	Memory
Kindness	Progression	Honor	Healing	Knowledge	Control

These are all powers Christ already possesses and is eager to share—in an elevated, sustainable, durable way. These powers will slowly increase within you until you eventually become all that God is.[4] President Nelson teaches us repeatedly about these powers because they are the inheritance of covenant keepers. When he teaches you to "think celestial," remember to be grateful to God, for it is His power that empowers you. And there's no better place to do this than in the temple, for as President Nelson taught, "Time in the temple will help you to think celestial and to catch a vision of who you really are, who you can become, and the kind of life you can have forever."

Time in the temple is power-generating because it triggers a higher level of partnership between you and Heavenly Father. Only then, when your priorities are selfless and consecrated, are you capable of getting what you really want in the most effective way. Only when you lose your life to Christ will you finally find a better life than you thought possible.

Heavenly Father is the best and only source of everything you really want. He is the best teacher for every ability. There is no other source of power as long-lasting or generous. Every other worldly source is a cheap imitation—small and bound to fail. The more you understand that God can offer you so much more than anyone or anything else, the better your life will be.

Is it selfish or improper to want all these godly powers? That's an important question, and it's part of the reason Christ refines your character slowly and sustainably. You must consistently demonstrate good stewardship and reliability. After being given a sampling of power, we all must succumb to God's all-knowing judgment. He will perceive your heart and determine whether you can be trusted with more of His power in the next life.

Yes, it is always improper to want these powers for your own glory, the way Satan did. At the beginning of the endowment ordinance, you will hear Heavenly Father deny Satan in premortality for this exact reason. However, having these powers forever is part of being like Christ, and it is never wrong to want to be like Him. In the endowment, you will also hear Christ commit Himself to Heavenly Father in selfless, consecrated service: "Here am I, send me" (Abraham 3:27). Only after committing His life to Heavenly Father was Christ given greater power and entrusted to become the Savior of the world.

If you sincerely honor God first in all things, desiring to serve Him and His children, then by covenant, He will help you develop His divine powers until you become a joint heir with Christ. These powers are part of your divine inheritance, accessed only by temple covenants. It is crucial to understand that this power-sharing process will only be done in God's way and in His timing. As He stated in scripture, "It is my purpose to provide for my saints, for all things are mine. But it must needs be done in mine own way" (Doctrine and Covenants 104:15–16).

A Firm Foundation: Fear Not

I have just emphasized to you that your Heavenly Father wants to grant you the best blessings and the greatest powers imaginable. That is a rather bold claim I'm making! God is offering you the most amazing deal of your eternal life. He is offering you what you want most while also offering protection from the fears that hold you back. Pray for confirmation if this is true. Only the Holy Ghost can convince you of such a significant promise.

Enduring to the end is an obstacle because you must believe that the promises are real while maintaining enough faith to overcome any impatience and distractions during mortality. Therefore, covenant guarantees are designed to help you feel more secure while you work patiently toward that good grade. After all, gold stars are usually given *after* a test, not in the middle of one.

Covenants do not prevent hardship. Instead, they help you stay focused on the true source of power so you can confidently continue forward. Making temple covenants is your opportunity to "walk on water" the way the Apostle Peter did.

Imagine a small boat full of tired, distressed disciples on the stormy Red Sea late at night (see Matthew 14:22–33). All evening, these experienced seamen had wrestled against the currents, unable to get to shore. In relief as well as disbelief, Peter saw Christ walking tall across the water. He wanted to be with Christ, to do what Christ could do. With Christ's call to "come," Peter stepped out of the boat. Miraculously, he walked! As if upheld by a firm foundation, Peter walked on the water.

For a moment, the churning sea does not lessen Peter's stability. But doubt set in as the winds and waves felt threatening and out of his control. Peter's vulnerability (or at least his belief that he is vulnerable) made him lose focus on Jesus. And because he doubted what he could do—and even doubted what *the Savior Himself would do*—Peter began to sink. Unable to swim by himself, he called out to Christ. Of course, Christ catches him by the hand. But He does not drag Peter through the water. Instead, Christ raises Peter up and walks with him over the water and back into the boat.

You, I, and Peter all need greater reassurance so that the winds and waves of life don't scare us from our goals. Temple covenants define what we can rely on. With awe and gratitude, I acknowledge that the list of blessings available through temple ordinances is quite long. These promises become the firm foundation we can confidently walk on, instead of sinking into despair, frustration, stress, or impatience.

It is so much easier to be a faithful covenant keeper if you truly believe that God can and will keep His promises. It is our vulnerabilities that lead us off the covenant path and into rough waters. People often make poor decisions under pressure, desperation, or the misguided fear of missing out on something better.

We sin because we rationalize it's the best way to get what we want. In fact, most sin is simply the result of trying to fulfill a righteous desire but in an ineffective, self-defeating way. We look for shortcuts because we lose focus or patience with God's way. I understand how tempting these shortcuts can be! But my point is that unrighteous shortcuts are absolutely unnecessary. Temple covenants offer the broader perspective you need to stay on track.

God wants to teach you how to achieve the desires of your heart just as much as you want to receive these desires. But He also wants to make sure you never lose these blessings. His covenant path is your best path forward (see 2 Nephi 9:41–43). This path is straight, meaning it is the most efficient path from one point to the next. This path is narrow. Could that also mean it is focused on the individual? No blessing of God will be denied to those who are faithful and patient covenant keepers, including those blessings that may feel the most out of reach for you personally.

Putting Christ first in your life is like learning to walk on water despite a sea of fears, difficulties, and even pain. Putting Christ last is like clinging to your boat in the middle of the stormy Red Sea while the currents toss you about.

Endowed with Power from on High

In the remainder of this book, I'm going to focus on the endowment covenants because they meld together to form the "firm foundation" of Christ (Helaman 5:12). Each covenant is one section of a bridge to Christ's power, with a built-in railing to stabilize you despite your vulnerabilities as you cross. Here is a brief overview of the five covenants taught in the temple, the promises I've come to associate with them, and the purpose each plays in Christ's power-sharing process:

The Law of Obedience
The promise of freedom, fairness, grace
How you RECOGNIZE Christ's power

The Law of Sacrifice
The promise of efforts being rewarded
How you GAIN Christ's power

The Law of the Gospel
The promise of love and redemption
How you KEEP Christ's power

The Law of Chastity
The promise of progress and added capability
How you INCREASE in Christ's power

The Law of Consecration
The promise to receive all God has and all God is
How you SHARE Christ's power

These five covenantal principles of the endowment are taught throughout scripture in poignant ways. Because Heavenly Father knew that these principles were so essential to His eternal, power-sharing process, He binds us to them through covenants.

For this power-sharing process to work, you need to learn some critical information:

- Who you are
- Where you came from
- Why God is worthy of your trust
- How the plan of salvation works
- What you need to do now (in mortality)
- How to get to the higher steps (in the spirit world)

All this information is taught to you on an elevated level during the endowment ordinance. Spend some time thinking about how the full endowment represents the plan of salvation, including the premortal life, mortal life, and afterlife. Here is a brief description of the separate parts.

The Initiatory Blessing

First, under priesthood authority, you are symbolically washed clean with a drop of water on your head, then anointed as royalty with a drop of oil. Next, you are given the most inspiring priesthood blessing, which describes in detail your promised status and abilities as an exalted covenant keeper. Finally, you are authorized to wear the garments of the holy priesthood with their protective power as you take on the name of Christ. The initiatory is a most wonderful gift from Heavenly Father.

The New Name

You are given a name that will act as a sacred key during your endowment ordinance. It is important that you always remember this name and live worthy to use it.

The Endowment

While the first two ordinances are offered individually, the endowment ordinance can be received by a large group at the same time. This portion currently takes just over one hour to complete. It includes a video depiction of the council in heaven, the Creation, and Adam and Eve's mortal experience. You will watch Adam and Eve learn about, make, and keep temple covenants as an example for all of us. The five endowment covenants are offered to you, and you are given the opportunity to accept them. As an act of service, a sacred prayer is given to request divine help for those people submitted through the prayer roll. Finally, a sacred highlight of the endowment ordinance comes during the veil ordinance. The veil of the temple represents Jesus Christ, His purpose, and His love for us.

The Celestial Room

To conclude, you are welcomed into the celestial room. In this sacred space, you can sit, ponder, and seek personal revelation. It is a place worthy of your divine identity and dedicated to inviting a closeness with God. It represents being with God and your heavenly family one day.

Higher Learning

The temple learning process is a beautiful metaphor for the plan of salvation. It makes me feel well cared for and purposeful. There is so much that could be said about each part, but the best way to learn is directly through the Holy Ghost. I have heard it said that the temple can speak for itself. Indeed, it has spoken to me.

Time in the temple refines you in a way that you cannot always define. It patches cracks and fills holes within your character from the inside out and outside in. Even those cracks you didn't know about or didn't know how to fix are slowly improving. Because I have spent hours and hours over years and years practicing my faults, it's reasonable to assume it will take significant time to heal them. But the promise is that they *can* be healed. My time in the temple has already proven quite productive in patching my cracks, and I'm confident yours will be too.

Chapter 2

The Creation

Michael

Soon to become Adam, the Father of All Living
The Archangel or Ancient of Days
On the sixth day of Creation, in the premortal life
See Genesis 1; Moses 2; and Abraham 4

So much has transpired, and so much more is yet to come.[5] I have labored at Jehovah's side and have marveled at His power, control, and care. His counsel and example have refined me. To mold in my hands the elements of life—to create solid structure for the support of glorious creatures—is exhilarating and joyful. To know that one day my children will walk the valleys I have formed, drink from the wells of water I have sprung, and marvel at the colors I have cultivated sustains me in this laborious and worthwhile effort.

I am overwhelmed with responsibility for my family—these many souls—who are relying on the detailed preparations I have made. But there is nothing more fulfilling than being given the highest tasks under the most critical pressures and still delivering for the ones you love most. Glory be given to God the Father and His Begotten Son for the opportunities and support they have offered me. From the deepest well of my soul, I love the work Father has given me to do.

The War in Heaven[6] carved a canyon through my heart—pain I thought might never be healed. I feel it every day, even now. A third of my brothers and sisters, destined to be my mortal sons and daughters, have suffered the only true death—separation from God, the end of progress. At the side of my brother, Jehovah, I have been given the largest task and the most experience of any of God's spirit children, so I know better than most the blessings these souls have lost and the good they could have done in mortality.

The wisps of doubt were so subtle at first—a quiet thought that maybe Christ wouldn't be strong enough to carry our sins or live perfectly. Then a hedging of doubt began to grow as others wanted the guarantee of return rather than the freedom of agency. But these spoken doubts, rationalizations, and justifications were only the outward shell of their true motivations. They dismissed the value of redemption and personal transformation within Father's well-established plan in favor of the selfish ease found in Lucifer's untested theory. Resentment bubbled to the surface over the necessity to test our agency before receiving glory equal to God's. Finally, a chasm formed between those who were relieved by the lack of responsibility and those who longed for progress.

Many lacked the understanding of how completely God would keep His promises. Satan downplayed the miracles of mortal life and exaggerated the pitfalls out of context. The storm of conflict grew beyond a matter of fear. It churned into corrupting pride, open rebellion, threatening distrust, and disregard for honor. The terrible harm that rebellious souls could inflict on earth became too great to ignore. By banishing Satan, the souls that followed him were made to understand that God would share His power only with those who had faith in Jesus Christ. In the end, with full knowledge of the plan of salvation, many followers of Lucifer chose to leave one by one.

I helped create the world, yet the greatest effort of my life has been to persuade my family to trust God and trust themselves. I strove valiantly, along with many others, to testify of the perfection of God's plan, the trust we held in Christ, and the hope we saw in the future. We taught and sustained all those around us. Following the example of our heavenly parents, we learned of their deep desires, explained how to achieve success, listened to their fears, and loved them. Every aspect of the plan was discussed, the necessity of every detail explained, as often as was required until every soul made a fully informed decision.

For one-third of us, it was a last act of pure agency. They chose voluntary entrapment rather than fulfilling the purpose of their premortal first estate (see Abraham 3:21–28). Their choices—and therefore their agency—would be restricted by the limitations they imposed on themselves.

I testify that after our mortal test, our ability, strength, and comprehension will far exceed what we currently possess here in the spirit. Currently, in this first estate, we know God's law and that it works, but we do not fully understand why. We do not fully understand what is required of a perfect God. Soon, we will have our own earthly experiences, granting us the wisdom that supersedes knowledge.

Deep in mourning for the loss of our family members, our heavenly parents had to embark on the next step of the plan of salvation. Completing the mighty task of Creation alongside Jehovah has brought healing to our broken hearts and confirmation of our victory.

Each step of Creation has had deep meaning and testified that God is love. Even in our grief, Creation has reinforced our resolve and reignited our excitement for the future.

On Day One, we laid the foundation upon which all other truths must be built: There is good, there is bad; there is light, there is dark. God, in His love and to His glory, has found a way to separate the two in the creation of the world, allowing us to thrive in His warm light rather than cower in the chaotic dark. We, His children, learned there is certainty in obediently choosing the good—it will always bring the light.

On Day Two, we separated heaven and earth and declared the difference between virtue and vanity. Virtuous choices lead to heavenly (eternal) blessings, while vain choices only lead to earthly (temporary) blessings. The cast of our grief was broken by remembering the wisdom in sacrificing now for greater benefits later.

On Day Three, we focused only on the necessities of life: a firm foundation, living water, shelter, sustenance, and progress. God understood our needs so completely. Christ directed me in the most detailed ways to fulfill the needs of our family. Truly, God understands that to choose well, our needs must be met. On this day, we learned that our devoted parents are the true source of all we need: love, balance, security, and nourishment.

Day Four was a day of hopes and dreams as we formed the great heavenly bodies that would become known as the sun, moon, and stars. The task just kept growing and growing and ever growing. Before we began, I had no comprehension of the lengths to which God would go for our benefit. I was so humbled by the effort He exhaustingly made for us that I wept tears of deep gratitude. Every deeply hidden fear was washed away by how much He loves us. Surely our greatest ambitions are not beyond God's power. We can trust Him!

After four grand days of practice and instruction, I was still intimidated by the task of Day Five to create the first creatures of the earth. I had learned what God could do, but didn't have enough faith in what I could do. Beginning simply, I had to work very slowly under Christ's careful instruction. Starting with the simplest of systems, I grew in skill and complexity. Practice and practice, repetition after repetition, till the systems were built for adaptation, sustainability, and procreation. This day emphasized how we are all being created by God. The Atonement of Jesus Christ will give us time in mortality to practice, develop, try again, and become perfected until Christ finally reigns and we achieve ever greater goals, line upon line.

On Day Six, while creating the first mammals, I reached the limits of my understanding. There was so much to consider and ponder. We were learning creation while also being taught by our creations. To see devotion in the paw of a mother bear, to see pursuit on the wing of an albatross, to see unity in the hive of a bee—all these things taught me deeply about my future role as the father of all living. The perpetuation of animal families sparked an exciting realization: We, too, could have tightly knit families of our own—families of belonging and partnership. The betrayal of the War in Heaven made our longing for devotion and loyalty all the stronger.

My part in Creation is finished for now. I have done all I can do. I have given the full limits of my capacity to my God in consecration. He has accepted my offering and, at each step along the way, called it good, though it was truly Him who magnified my efforts beyond what I could have done alone.

As a supernal gift, before the end of the sixth day, my physical body and the body of mighty Eve will be created in the image of our heavenly parents. It will be a task so sacred that even Jehovah cannot do it alone. Of all the beauty that could be created, our bodies will be the crowning achievements. We truly are the heritage of gods.

It is nearly finished! God is nearly done with all He promised to do. The Day of Rest will be as magnificent as the seraphic hosts of heaven declare that God truly does keep His promises! Throughout mortality, every seventh day will commemorate this powerful truth.

But I will not be here to see these heavenly celebrations.

Now comes a most difficult choice. The plan cannot go forward unless I decide to leave our heavenly home—to start my mortal journey as Adam, to begin as a lone man in the Garden of Eden. Above all else, the greatest desire of my heart is to be with my Father and my Savior (see Moses 5:10). I have been granted the honor of working closely at Their side. I have witnessed firsthand Their glory. Nothing can ever compare. And yet I must choose to separate myself from what I want the very most. Indeed, I must be the first to do so, and I must do so twice! Right now, I must give up Their presence while basking in Their glory. Then in the garden, I must again give up Their presence while feeling my own vulnerabilities.

It is contrary to my very being to leave Them—but I must if I am ever to learn to choose correctly in a fully independent way. I am foreordained to one day vanquish Satan for good, but only if I choose now to learn how (see Doctrine and Covenants 88:112–15).

I must begin now to set a brave example as a father. Our God has loved me so deeply that I can, with confidence, give up what brings me incredible joy, knowing that I will again see my God with my physical eyes. My physical body must learn the benefits of obedience if my physical powers are going to be used honorably.

I know that He gives direction one day at a time, one step at a time. I know that God is creating me into a more powerful son. Even after leaving the Garden of Eden, I know I will feel again the satisfaction of hearing God declare my work to be good.

Eve

The Mother of All Living
First Female Child of God
After leaving the Garden of Eden
See Moses 3–5

I have a memory that will bring me warmth when I am cold and comfort when I am lost. It is a memory that God prepared ahead of time because He knew me and He knew Adam. It testifies to Father's forethought and understanding.

I remember the first time I looked into Adam's eyes. They were filled with wonder and gratitude, relief and openness, because these were the eyes of a man who knew what loneliness felt like. It created a willingness in Adam to fully cleave himself to me in body, mind, and soul. He has never sought the upper hand. His wish has ever been to just hold my hand.

Wanting to share eagerly in partnership, he cherished my place in the garden and helped me understand how unity was required to keep any of God's commandments. Our time in the garden was spent developing our love and understanding of one another and of our Father until we wanted to seal ourselves in companionship as helpmeets under His authority.

I could not have faced this unknown world without Adam's commitment to me and our future family. But I had to make my choice independently, because the choice of selflessness cannot be made by anyone else.

Adam also needed the opportunity to make his own choice. When I presented the forbidden fruit and my choice to Adam, there was a moment when my memory flashed back to our first meeting. Would he understand the importance of us remaining together? Would Adam recognize that we must remain united to fulfill God's purposes?

As I tearfully looked into his eyes, anticipating his reaction, I again saw that look of committed partnership. He already understood that man must not be alone. He already yearned for a family as deeply as I did. Adam was an immortal in paradise, but he chose to be mortal with me instead. By taking the fruit himself, he was witnessing unto

God that we, when sealed together in unity (see Moses 3:22–25), were willing to start an independent family despite the sacrifices required.

As never before, we can now fulfill the measure of our creation. Upon taking these first steps of independence, we have graduated from the sanctuary of the garden, but not without first being gifted great tools of protection and reassurance to counter our vulnerabilities.

Vulnerability can be such a powerful emotion, one that can even make you forget the comfort and peace you always enjoyed. I felt it first when I was unsure of what would become of us. Our Father is ever loving and wise yet supremely fair. He warned us we would have to leave if we ate the fruit, but would I ever see Him again? Even the thought was nearly unbearable. How could our Father balance our need for independence and our need for Him?

I felt vulnerability a second time when Lucifer introduced us to shame and then left to hide himself away. In pointing out our nakedness, he made me feel that I should have known better. I was confused and unsure about myself—feelings I had never experienced or been taught by my Father. Never once had He made me feel shame despite the youthfulness of my understanding. Godly sorrow brings the desire to do better, while shame only elicits a desire to hide.

Always with an answer, our Father taught us of the redeeming role our brother, Jehovah, will play. How divine is Jehovah to die willingly so that my family can fully live! I will return to my Father because Jehovah will make it so. I feel so responsible for the sacrifice He will need to make. But Jehovah has reassured me of His choice. Face-to-face, He has promised to redeem me and my children from our sins. We all understand there is no other way we can all be together again. My heart trembles with gratitude for my Savior and His act of Atonement.

To protect us from this feeling of shame, Father has gifted us coats of skin. He explained how they serve as a constant reminder of Jehovah's atoning sacrifice for our mistakes and the promises of our future. His sacrifice of my beloved Elder Brother will free me from the unfairness of shame because of what I do not yet understand. It will grant me the safety needed while I recognize weakness, feel godly sorrow, desire to learn better, and complete the work I need to do. These garments will remind me that God loves me daily and that my success remains intact despite my inevitable missteps. They will also protect me from the powers of Lucifer so that he cannot manipulate me again unless I let him. The threats of Lucifer still ring in my ears and overshadow my future family, but these protective garments grant me the courage to do what is good and right. They remind me that Father is stronger than Lucifer, and also that I am stronger than Lucifer if I am covenanted with Father.

Finally, Father has also gifted us with the law of obedience. He has promised to give us teachers to guide us further and to give us whatever strength we need to make the right choices. Just as in the garden, we will continually have the freedom to choose for ourselves. If we seek His help, it will be available. If we don't, He will respect our wishes. We can return only if we choose.

I am leaving this beautiful home, this garden created just for us, but it is not without preparation. I have the very best of partners. I have the very best support. Finally, I can learn like never before, love like never before, and grow like never before. Finally, I have the chance to fulfill my plan of salvation (see Moses 5:11).

God Is Still Creating You

I would love to know more about Adam and Eve. We focus so much on the beginning of their story without realizing that their exceptionally long lives were full of daily mini-steps of progress. They are examples of progress made. We can look to them and see ourselves learning, developing, and improving slowly but sustainably year by year.

God knows how important it is for us to remain confident in the plan of salvation, so He reminds us every Sabbath day during the sacrament that He will keep His promises. Keeping your promises to Him is the most important factor in reaching your life goals.

Throughout the Creation, Christ went to our Father and was given direction sufficient for that day. Every day, Christ was provided what He needed to take the next step. Every day, Christ proved His obedience. Day by day, He learned to use the power given to Him in ways that would increasingly benefit His whole family.

Heavenly Father is teaching you in the same way. Every day, you can go to Heavenly Father in prayer, with a goal in mind, and be provided with direction sufficient for the next small step forward. You can have the confirmation of the Spirit that your daily work is good, even if your full creation process is still unfinished.

God first created our world. His next goal is to prepare us for His power. The baptism, priesthood, endowment, and sealing covenants build us up the same way the seven days of Creation built up the world.

Our covenants mark the major steps along Jacob's covenant ladder—but layered throughout are all the daily mini-steps that transform us into increasingly capable children of God. Just as Christ did, you can make goals day by day. You can watch your ennobling progress and witness God create ever better opportunities. Your trust in your Savior and your eagerness to partner with Him will grow.

Be Not Afraid

I am sure Adam and Eve felt anxious and trepidation as they walked into the unknown, uncontrolled world outside the protection of the Garden of Eden. But God prepared them for what they would face. He gifted them the knowledge of their Savior, garments of protection, the Adamic language of power, covenants of promise, and the guidance of heavenly messengers.

Heavenly Father creates a covenant relationship with them and with you, so you don't need to be afraid either. One-third of the host of heaven chose Satan because deep down, they were scared of something. God does not want you to be afraid of anything. Covenants counteract our mortal vulnerabilities and fears that slow our progress. Consider what the five covenants teach us:

1. The Law of Obedience—God will never betray you, unfairly judge you, or abandon you.
2. The Law of Sacrifice—God will only lead the best way.
3. The Law of the Gospel—God will love you perfectly and grant you grace.
4. The Law of Chastity—God will be the eternal source of increasing power.
5. The Law of Consecration—God will help you become like Him.

Each covenant builds on the next to calm your fears and increase your hopes. In a worldwide devotional to young adults, President Nelson promised five grand outcomes to those who keep their temple covenants:

1. Strength to keep your covenants
2. Freedom from fear
3. More confidence than you can currently imagine
4. Positive influence far beyond your capacity
5. An exhilarating future[7]

Do you see the connection between each covenant and each prophetic promise? I stand amazed that these blessings are just a sample of what is offered to you through temple covenants. Each of the five covenants (obedience, sacrifice, the gospel, chastity, and consecration) meld together to create a firm foundation upon which to steady your fears and build your hopes.

Chapter 3

The Law of Obedience

Nephi

Youngest son of Lehi and Sariah
Camped in the Valley of Lemuel
See 1 Nephi 2–3

We've been out in the open desert for several weeks now. Only by pure miracle did we find this ribbon of green in the shallow of a riverbed flowing with fresh water. Our trek has been nothing but shrubs, lifeless swaths of bedrock, and blowing sand. There's enough water here to sustain us for our journey onward. There are even a few trees big enough to shade our tents. Watering the animals, washing in the water, and spotting signs of game, we all felt rescued but continued to wonder what would come next.

As a child, the open desert scared me. How many times had I heard of someone who didn't survive here? One of my worst fears came true when my father woke me so early in the morning to tell me we had to leave Jerusalem and never return.

I gathered, I packed, and I left.

But what else was I going to do? I really only had two choices. Neither was what I wanted, but it was the reality of my situation. I could stay and be captured by the Babylonians, or I could follow

God's direction and escape. At least God told us what to expect and how to survive.

The right choice was obvious. My brothers didn't see that their complaints were just a waste of effort. They could stay if they wanted, but why would they? Why did they think they could debate the reality that there were ten Babylonian soldiers for every one of ours? Were they deaf to the harassment growing ever more frequent? For millennia, the only reason Jerusalem survived constant threats was because God had made it so. Since God wasn't planning another miraculous rescue, we had to leave.

I now must trust the voice that warned us in the first place. I know being with God is better than being on my own because God told us exactly what to do. By contrast, our feckless king, Zedekiah, won't admit what is coming. He couldn't prevent it if he wanted to. My tribal patriarchs are ruthless, selfish, and utterly incapable of protecting us. Our friends and neighbors are no match for the Babylonians. Even my older brothers are unreliable. To believe I had any other source of protection would be foolish. Only my God through His prophet could protect me, and He always has.

My childish nightmare of the desert has become my lived experience these past few weeks. But God provided this oasis, didn't He? And it hasn't been that bad. Instead of just waiting to see what terrible thing might happen next, I have a way to know that I will be saved no matter what. In a way, God has given me control of my outcome because I get to choose whether I obey His direction. If I follow the Lord, He will protect me, teach me, and guide me, or else bring me home to Him. Either way, I will be well. Why would I want to choose anything else?

My father called me into his tent this morning. He was standing tall and proud, the way he does when I know I'm talking to a prophet, not just my father. But this time, when he looked at me, I caught him glancing downward. He was worried about something. I think it must have been because he wasn't sure how I would respond to what he had to say. His doubt made me feel exposed to a different kind of danger.

He asked me to return all the way back to Jerusalem to get plates of scripture that contained the teachings of the Christ.

In that moment, my weaknesses felt so obvious. I don't know anything about navigation, negotiation, or leadership. I felt so small. But after a moment, the faith in my heart challenged the prick of doubt in my mind. Knowing what God wanted me to choose made me feel stronger and more confident. I can't say I was eager, but I was willing.

I chose to do as Christ had asked because I know Christ has chosen to lead me. I trust that there must be a good reason He has asked me to do this, so I'm not going to argue with the God who has already saved me once. My father prophesied that the Lord would not suffer those who come unto Him to perish (see 1 Nephi 1:14). If I believe in His tender mercies, then I'm going to have to believe He'll protect me.

Despite my willingness, the words I spoke unto my father were not my own. It was as if God controlled my mouth to speak the words I needed to hear. Years from now, I will need to remember what I said to my father on this day. I engraved these words in my mind:

"I will go and do the things which the Lord hath commanded, for I know that the Lord giveth no commandments unto the children of men, save *he shall prepare a way for them that they may accomplish* the thing which he commandeth them" (1 Nephi 3:7; emphasis added).

Accomplishment—that is what I want, and that is what God has offered me.

The deep relief I saw on my father's face surprised me. He suddenly looked so aged. I thought about what he must be feeling: he is the only one who can lead this family; he is the only one who holds the priesthood keys; he is the only one to whom God revealed this plan; there is no one else to carry the burden but him.

My father is leading us further away from what we know and probably feeling older every day. My brothers would crumble under such pressure. Laman and Lemuel can't be leaders like my father because they believe in their fears more than they believe in their God. There's no reason Sam couldn't, but he just doesn't. Who else will save my family? I guess my father is relying on me. He did call me into the tent first this morning, probably because he wants me to help my brothers understand.

There is no one else to lead my family unless I choose to learn how. Again, why would I make any other choice? I don't want to fail. I don't want to die. Even more so, I want my family to live. Christ promised I could go and do this . . . so I will.

Why didn't we get these plates before we left Jerusalem? The question has filled my mind all day, as if God wants me to find an answer. I walked along the river for a long way until I was far out of sight. I knelt and asked.

Pieces of ideas filtered through my mind till one appeared to be written in gold. Maybe God has been preparing me for today ever since we left Jerusalem. Nearly every step from there to here, I have been rehashing the reasons why we are here and why we are doing this. God warned us . . . God wants us to live ... God loves us ... I trust Him.

The tedious walking hasn't been unproductive after all. I believe what God says. It got me ready for what my father was going to say today. I've crossed a threshold. The Holy Ghost has spoken confidence in my heart.

I think this is how Christ will teach me to be the leader my family needs me to be.

Promises Received Through Obedience

Sometimes God shows us intense examples in the scriptures. For me, they illustrate the great adaptability of God's promises. God's covenant principles are eternally correct—even in the direst of circumstances.

Nephi had to make an urgent choice in an intense situation: follow His prophet into the wilderness or remain in Jerusalem under threat by one of the most brutal armies ever known. It's important to remember that Nephi could have made either choice. But Nephi's writings emphasize there is no point in making an unrighteous choice, because what you truly want is achieved only through Christ.

Human progress, modern comforts, and cultural norms all camouflage the fact that you are also facing a choice just as consequential as Nephi's: repent of your sins through the Atonement of Jesus Christ, or follow Satan, the greatest threat to your peace and happiness. There are only two choices. Heavenly Father and Jesus Christ are so patient with you as you learn this concept. Still, Their patience doesn't change the reality of the situation that there are only two options to choose from.

This is a difficult truth to accept because it understandably evokes a lot of fear. For example:

- What if you don't want to do what is asked of you?
- What if it's hard to tell the difference between right and wrong?
- What if you don't understand why it's being asked?
- What if you can't seem to do it?
- What if there are other things to do that simply make much more sense?
- What if the gospel is just a big lie?

There is a fear at the root of each of these questions. These fears are precisely why God made obedience a *covenant*, not just a commandment. A covenant is a binding two-way promise with an all-powerful God. Now all your questions can be answered with guarantees (if you keep your covenants and follow Christ) in even the most extreme circumstances.

Obedience is the first covenant of the temple endowment. All five covenants work together, but the first one lays the ground rules that all the others build on. Therefore, it's important to understand it and have faith in how it works. Is it any surprise that the first book of the Book of Mormon highlights Nephi learning these lessons by living them?

1. Christ offers His grace so that the choice to obey is not beyond your ability (1 Nephi 3:7).
2. Heavenly Father is mighty and does not make mistakes (1 Nephi 4:1–3).
3. The Holy Ghost sees both your actions and your intentions clearly (1 Nephi 4:10–11).
4. Heavenly Father gives the best rewards (1 Nephi 15:36).
5. Through the Atonement of Jesus Christ, your test will be judged fairly and in a perfectly customized way (2 Nephi 9:14–15).

Nephi and many other prophets have explained key principles about obedience found within the scriptures. Applying these principles as a covenant contract between you and Heavenly Father reveals significant benefits of comfort.

Covenant Principle	Covenant Benefit
Obedience will always be your choice (2 Nephi 2:27–30).	Your need for freedom is respected.
Obedience is requested by a perfect God (Hebrews 5:8–9).	Your mortal test will be judged fairly.
Obedience will always be within your ability (1 Corinthians 10:13).	Your Savior will always support you.

- **Freedom:** Obedience will always be your free and willing choice. Obedient choices will always lead to more freedom. "I, the Lord God, make you free, therefore ye are free indeed; and the law also maketh you free" (Doctrine and Covenants 98:8).
- **Fairness:** Christ will ensure that your personal journey of obedience is fair and tailored, despite the ripple effects caused by flawed mortal men and women. "I will go and do the things which the Lord hath commanded, for I know that the Lord giveth no commandments unto the children of men, save he shall prepare a way for them that they may accomplish the thing which he commandeth them" (1 Nephi 3:7).
- **Success:** Christ will provide you the help you need to ensure that spiritual success is always within your power to achieve. "And again I say unto you, if ye observe to do whatsoever I command you, I, the Lord, will turn away all wrath and indignation from you, and the gates of hell shall not prevail against you" (Doctrine and Covenants 98:22).

Irrevocably Decreed

In return for these benefits, you promise to have faith in Jesus Christ, honor your baptismal covenants, obey the commandments, seek the personal guidance of the Holy Ghost, and follow the teachings of the prophet with any endurance necessary.

It also means that you obey the deeper spirit of His laws, not just the letter of His laws. For example, you should do more than just pay your tithing in gratitude to Heavenly Father. You must also take part in the sacrament, do missionary work, and attend the temple.

The law of obedience implies a recognition that Christ is more intelligent than you (see Abraham 3:19). But it also opens yet another access point for Christ to bless you. As Doctrine and Covenants 130:20–21 teaches us, "There is a law, irrevocably decreed in heaven before the foundations of this world, upon which all blessings are predicated—And when we obtain any blessing from God, it is by obedience to that law upon which it is predicated."

- **Irrevocable:** A perfect word to describe God's side of a covenant. It means guaranteed. It means not even Christ has the power to change it (not that He would want to).
- **Predicated:** This word means "based on," "tied to," or "linked." The law of obedience always triggers blessings because there is a guaranteed cause-and-effect relationship. The covenant of obedience goes a step further. Now it is a personal commitment between you and Heavenly Father. Christ's help will be customized to fit *your* needs, and His blessings will be customized to help you get what *you* want.

Fears about obedience will come up. They do for everyone. Please remember that the personal freedoms you are worried about are seen and respected. Obedience would not be asked of you unless it led to what God knows you want. As you recognize Christ's help, let it calm your mortal fears.

Most importantly, obedience is the first step toward God's goal of helping you become personally fulfilled and joyful. He will not betray you or compromise your joyful outcome. If His answer is no, it is probably because you would choose no if you had His foresight.

How to Recognize Christ's Power

As you keep the law of obedience, Christ will be more active in your life because you have authorized Him to do more for you. The more obedient you are, the better you will *recognize* His power making a difference in your success. As you make obedient choices, you will *see* evidence of His gospel and wisdom interacting toward your improvement.[8]

Day by day, you can begin to trust Christ's guidance not just in your spiritual learning but also in your choices, relationships, goals, and hardships. Slowly but surely, your spiritual experiences through Christ accumulate. Over time, there is no denying that He is real and active in your life. His interactions will affect even the critical hinge points in your life, altering your outcomes for the better.

My experience with obedience has not been smooth. When I was younger, I wanted to do things my own way. I didn't need anyone's help. I wasn't satisfied with the righteous lives around me, so why would I copy what they had done? So I didn't. And guess what happened? Nothing. Nothing particularly good anyway. I wasn't doing anything too bad, but I didn't feel particularly good either. I was not making decisions with the intent or desire to follow God's direction; I only wanted to rely on my own perceptions. I was coasting—tiring, numbing, aimless coasting. At times, I felt like I was floundering, then regret would settle in. But I still pretended I was successful. I didn't have much control over my future, so I didn't have much confidence in it either. I was guessing, then waiting to see if it worked out okay. I was certainly trying to be proactive, but my plans were only my best *guess* of what I should do.

At one critical hinge point in my life, the Holy Ghost spoke up loudly and directed my success. At age 19, I moved to New York City with my older siblings and secured a job working at the personal investment firm of billionaire Michael Dell. Life was exciting and happily far away from my sleepy life in Arizona. Feeling rather adult-like during this first mini-step of independence, I wanted to determine for myself whether the Church of Jesus Christ was true. So I tested the Spirit by changing my habits to be more obedient and spiritually intentional.

I remember the day I read Apostle Paul's description of seeing through a glass darkly (see 1 Corinthians 13:11–13). I realized that was something I was afraid of—making decisions based on bad information. I was also worried about making choices and not being able to foretell the bad outcomes that could follow. I wanted more control, and I knew I couldn't get it by myself. So my choices became more intentionally faith-filled.

A few months later, clear promptings from the Holy Ghost kept coming. Multiple times, I had the feeling that I was supposed to go home. I didn't want to go. I didn't understand why. I certainly wouldn't have made that choice myself.

Finally, I went to my boss and gave my resignation. She didn't understand it either. They liked me, had promoted me twice already, and didn't understand why I would want to leave. She offered me more money. I declined. She offered me paid tuition. I declined again. But this time, it was as if the words were not my own: God needed me to go home. With gratitude and apologies, I left.

Long story short, I went out with my future husband just after arriving home. We married and were surprised by an immediate pregnancy. It was startling to so quickly go from a Fifth Avenue corporate penthouse to changing diapers in less than two years. My intentions for law school no longer felt like the right choice for me either.

Fast forward a few more short years, and I recognized the reason for the Spirit's intervention. I lost my ability to have children. If the Holy Ghost hadn't directed a customized path for me, I wouldn't have my three daughters. I might have more money, a law degree, and a prestigious job, but I would not have what I treasure most.

God allowed me a taste of the lifestyle I thought I wanted, probably because I am stubborn and hard-headed. But then, they customized a path for me to choose a much better outcome. Because of obedience, my family and I benefited from Christ's power of foresight, grace, and empowerment.

Your direction will look very different from mine, but that is why it's so valuable. Obedience can help you *recognize* Christ's personalized direction. Please trust the direction He gives you.

You can't control most things, but you *can* control whether you partner with Christ. He has the power to control your success. Therefore, obedience saves you from making life harder than it needs to be. You can pair Almighty God's abilities with your own. The prophet Jeremiah described it this way: "Behold, as the clay is in the potter's hand, so are ye in mine hand, O house of Israel" (Jeremiah 18:6).

With full agency, and only if you want Him to, Christ is offering to craft your life with the skill of the Master Artist. And He can do this much better than you can by yourself.

Like the blind man whom Christ healed (see John 9:6–7), earthly temptation and distraction are covering your eyes like mud. As you obey the direction to go and wash away your earth-stains, you can look up to *see* Him. The next step toward what you want most will become clearer, Christ's power will become more evident, and His wisdom will become more comprehensible to you.

Chapter 4

The Law of Sacrifice

Sam

Brother of Nephi
Sailing in the open ocean toward the promised land
See 1 Nephi 18

I'm in a dark, dank hull being tossed by a monstrous sea. There is a storm just as fierce churning in my mind. My children are crying in fear, trapped in a ship that could break apart at any moment. My wife is holding our baby as tightly as she can, crouched between a post and a barrel. I am bruised and bleeding, attempting to comfort them. Everyone I love in the world could die tonight.

How did I get into this wretched situation? I followed the direction of my God. I do not say so in a mocking way; I am just being honest. I can be realistic and faithful at the same time. I lost my home, but will receive the promised land. My brothers beat me, but an angel proved that God is on my side. I held my wife while she bore our children in a filthy tent, but I witnessed her strength equal to my own. Great leaps of understanding and progress mark each sacrifice as God stretches me and propels me forward.

I feel such a flood of hate for my eldest brother that I fear it may drown me. His betrayal, his violence! My anger sends cracks of lightning across my thoughts, while my understanding of God answers with a roll of thunder. The two have been competing in my mind as the storm outside has grown ever more dangerous.

Laman, Lemuel, and the sons of Ishmael have been the embodiment of opposition. They struggle to obey, so at each sacrifice, they struggle to trust. They cannot release control to God despite all His power. They cannot see that righteousness works better.

My elder brothers have risked the destruction of all our families by tying Nephi to a mast. Doing so is a sign of cowardice and indecision. If they were not afraid of God's punishment, they would just kill him. If they were not afraid of priesthood power, they would lock Nephi up below. So instead, what is their plan? Leave Nephi tied for months while they attempt to sail back.

It's madness, this storm is proof. But wickedness has never been reasonable. Nephi is close to dying. I can feel it. Once again, I know I must climb that ladder to beg for the life of my brother and all our family. But what will I do when Laman refuses once again? I shake the thoughts from my head.

My legs are shaky after being cramped and cold for so long. The ship is heaving, throwing me off balance. My wife watches me, immediately shaking her head.

"No, no! We could be separated if you go up there."

"Do you want me to stay when I feel God asking me to go?" Crouching down to where she sits, I kneel and kiss the top of her head. She grabs my arm and pulls me in close. I hear her crying in the dark. We don't say goodbye even though we know it could be goodbye.

Making my way to the ladder, I pass my children, my parents, my brothers, and my sisters. They have given their all for this journey. I walk by Lemuel's three-year-old son. He is crying out for his mother, too far away to reach. I cradle his head in my hand and tell him everything will be better soon. Then I ascend the ladder and look up through the hatch at the storm raging above me.

Do I stay or do I go? Do I leave the fate of my family in the hands of Laman, or do I take action myself? This is a hinge point I cannot return from as the same man. God wants me up above, but I may throw

Laman overboard if I go. It is just as likely that Laman may throw me overboard. I cannot foresee what God has in mind.

For years, Laman and Lemuel bullied and scorned me with unwavering disdain. I know why: I have been able to do what they cannot. I feel enabled by the leadership of our younger brother, Nephi, while they can only feel diminished.

Laman rages against Nephi's leadership, while I respect Nephi's service. No one has worked harder, no one has been more focused than Nephi. Nephi leads because Nephi serves, while Laman can't even see the need for service. Nephi needs me now, so I exit the hatch at the center of the main deck.

The onslaught of water is more than I expected. Sea water and rain are coming down in sheets. But I know where I need to go. The wind is whipping at my hair and howling past my ears. I steady myself against the main mast, then stumble my way to the front. I'm not feeling a sense of peace or confidence. I'm feeling dread. The fury in my heart is heating me up, distracting me from what's more important.

I can hear two of Ishmael's sons on the quarter deck up behind me. It sounds like it takes all their strength to control the wheel against the current. Lemuel is the first person I see.

"Get back below!" he snarls at me.

Lemuel can't hide it. He is feeling guilty and terrified, I can tell. He knows the situation is out of his control.

"Do you think I will survive down there? Do you think your family will survive down there?" I counter back.

With both arms, Lemuel reaches for me to push me back toward the hatch, but I am angrier than he expects. For hours, my fists have been clenched. My arms have ached for a chance to lay into Laman and Lemuel, stronger than I have ever felt before. With one hard, fast strike, I aim for the side of his lower back, just where I know it will hurt him most. His upper body wrenches backward, and his knees give out. The ship pitches up at an odd angle, backing me up against the quarterdeck, but Lemuel spills forward and tumbles against the railing further down the gangway.

I keep moving forward and climb the steps to the foredeck. Ishmael's oldest son, Mathoni, is challenging Laman with a knife. I don't know whether Mathoni is trying to free Nephi or to take control of the ship. Someone has to stop Laman, and I'm happy for anyone to give it a try. I can see cuts on Laman's arms even as he taunts Mathoni for more. Never in my life have I seen Laman back away from a fight. Stumbling like a drunken man, he lunges back at Mathoni, challenging him to try again.

How can we take a man like this to the promised land? I see the churning seas and the dark sky. I hear the creaking of the ship and the snapping of the lines. This storm is Laman's fault! I blame him for my fear and for this danger. I watch as Mathoni swings his arm in a deadly arch toward my own brother—and in my heart, I hope Mathoni is the better fighter.

He misses by inches, but I won't. Tearing a heavy piece of wood from a broken crate, I make my way up toward the fight. While Laman and Mathoni are circling back to face one another again, I finally see Nephi at the foremast. He's slumped against ropes, tied like an animal.

Sensing my chance to take Laman down, I run forward, weapon in hand. I pour my anger and frustration into that swing and aim for the back of Laman's head.

At the last moment, Nephi calls out. "Sam, no!"

Laman instinctively ducks as my swing passes by. Turning to me, he rams his shoulder into my chest and we both struggle to stay upright.

A threat was rising from behind but we didn't see it coming. A rogue wave crashes over the side of the ship and spills onto the deck. The water washes out my legs, and I'm smashed into stacks of wooden boxes tied to the deck. Laman tumbles down hard.

The knife gone, Laman is left moaning on the ground. Sensing that the storm has grown into a bigger threat, Mathoni leaves to find his brothers. Surely, Laman will relent now. This storm is increasing in intensity. How little I understand the irrationality of pride!

Laman is hardly back on his feet before he crashes on top of me.

"The ship is mine. Get below!"

"Let him go, Laman," I yell, half-shocked.

"I will not!" he bellows. "Nephi will not lead us again."

"Then we will die, led by no…"

I don't finish. Pitching forward then back, the ship is rising through the air to the crest of a wave, only to dive down the other side. I lunge back to the boxes secured to the deck, seeing another monstrous wave growing over our heads. This next wave will scatter everything that's not tied down. I don't warn Laman, I don't reach for him. I twist to make sure Nephi is still secured to the mast. Is it ironic that Nephi may be the safest person on the boat?

Time is running out. The wave is upon us. I slide my body under the ropes and hold on. The head of the giant wave crashes upon the deck. For a moment, I'm completely underwater until we begin to fall the remaining slope of the wave.

I look to my left in just enough time to see the bowsprit crack and flip backward onto the deck. It splinters, leaving a jagged hole. I cover my head and turn to my right. I see Laman haul himself back over the railing. He must have come so close to his own destruction!

I untangle myself, get up, and run for the mast to try to untie Nephi.

"Sam, what are you doing?"

"Untying you, Nephi!"

"You could have killed Laman!"

"He is about to kill us all!"

"You're only adding to the storm, Sam." What did he say? His words pierced the cold and drowned out the wind. Instead, I heard the cries of my children in my ears, and I saw the little face cradled in my hand moments ago. Could I be partly responsible for the waves strong enough to swamp our ship and crack the hull?

Laman is on me before I can make much progress. Too soon, another sizable wave spills over the side. I bury my face into Nephi's shoulder and wrap my arms through the extra ropes even as Laman is trying to break my hold. Again, the crush of the water, but this time it pins me against the mast and hurls Laman around the side as the boat leans over dangerously far. One rope is the only thing that keeps Laman from washing overboard. Watching Laman look so precarious, eyes just as scared as mine would be, I suddenly remembered something important—his humanity and my own.

As the wave recedes, we catch our breath and my brothers are both right up close. Even with the roar of the storm, they can hear me.

"Nephi, you will live. Because of Laman's opposition, you have held ever tighter to the Lord."

Laman stares at me.

"Laman, you will die. This storm is stronger than you. Let him go! There will be no Laman without Nephi."

From the hole in the foredeck, we can hear terrified screams echoing up from the hull below.

"Do you hear them, Laman? Those cries for help are your children; that is your family."

Suddenly, the boat smacks hard against the sea's surface, and Laman is knocked loose from his hold of the mast. Water surges up on all sides of the ship. That quickly, Laman is just sucked away. No chance to grab his hand or see his face. He is just gone.

My heart sinks to the bottom of the sea. The water recedes, but still I don't see him.

"Where is he?" Nephi calls out, unable to see behind.

Half a wail catches in my throat as I collapse against the mast. Am I shocked by my loss or the stubbornness of Laman's betrayal?

"Laman!" My scream hardly comes out. "Laman!"

I let go of the mast, the only thing that had kept me from being swept into the dark water. I run for the railing and search the water. The sea has caught him, and Laman is being pulled away from us.

Has this not always been the case? As a family, we have been anchored by our belief in Christ, yet he has floated out into a sea of misconceptions. As a family, we have offered a haven, yet he has rejected it, wanting instead to do things his way. Now more than ever, he is utterly alone.

My mind is racing. I have spent years hating Laman, and yet at this moment, why do I want him back? Because he has value to God or because he has value to me? If I knew I would lose my family on this journey, would I have still come? Yes, because we are ever in the hands of Christ! Then why can't I extend that faith toward Laman? Christ is stronger than Laman's opposition. Why am I so afraid of what Laman can do that I was willing to reject Christ's commandments to solve this problem my own way? Does the Lord not know what He is doing? I should never have hoped for Laman's death.

I search the deck for the stray ropes and throw the coil toward Laman as hard as I can.

"Dear Lord, forgive me. Extend Thy grace! Please! Mercy, Lord!"

Even as my hope begins to fade, Laman sees me and grabs hold of the rope. I race back to the foremast where Nephi has been calling for me, and I entangle the ropes again around my arms. As the next wave spills over the side, I'm distracted trying to keep the loose bowsprit from ramming into us.

By the time I turn back to the railing, I see Lemuel hauling what I'm sure is Laman back onto the ship. I take the chance to say a prayer of gratitude that no one has yet died from this catastrophe.

Laman, exhausted but on board, stumbles toward us. He stops short as he scans Nephi. Even as we brace ourselves against a smaller wave, Laman's stark white face can't look away from what he has done. He cannot unhear the calls for help from below. Every muscle in his body clenches as he screams out in frustration, hands tight-fisted, eyes looking wildly for any other alternative.

Lemuel comes up behind him, but Laman shoves him away. I can almost see the internal battle between his pride, his fears, his love for us, and his sense of self-preservation. Fuming with defeat, but utterly spent, he turns away. But that won't be good enough to stop this God-given storm, so I can't let Laman go.

Forgiveness and a complete trust in Christ have been a sacrifice I have been unwilling to give. I feel filthy for the dirty hatred I have held in my heart for so long. I rush at Laman, grabbing his arm, fighting an internal battle of my own. The actions of my body and the thoughts in my head don't align. I pull his face up to mine, my voice rising in intensity.

"I have hated you. I have cursed you. I have wished for your death. But I must carve this anger out of me if we are going to survive this storm!" I shove his arm away and take a step back.

"Will you forgive me, Laman? I want you with us, brother! I understand better the dangers of pride. It makes you feel strong even though you are small. Real strength is the power of God." My tone softens, and my arms drop.

"We may die tonight and yet I forgive you, Laman, for what you have brought upon us and our families."

Dumbstruck, Laman stares into my face and takes a few steps backward along the gangway as Lemuel yells out a warning. The ship drops hard against the surface, and water is again forced up all sides. The sea grabs me with enough force to pull me overboard.

I don't understand what happened. I don't know how he got there so fast. At the last moment, Laman's hand grabs mine. He lies back low, bracing his legs against the railing and anchoring me to the deck.

Landing in a pile, we are both breathing hard.

"I couldn't let you die like that, Sam."

"We will all die like that, Laman, if you don't repent." Kneeling there on the deck, pelted with rain, looking out at the gauntlet of never-ending waves, Laman takes some shallow breaths and then covers his face in his hands. Knowing another wave could come at any moment, Laman begins to pray silently. Holding still, I watch him. He raises his arms toward God. They are shaking and fall quickly, but Laman has relented. I know what this has cost him and what it has earned him. He will be given another chance.

Though the rains are still pounding and the ship is still pitching, no other wave pours over the ship as Laman cuts away Nephi's bindings. Now freed, I catch Nephi from falling and hold him up on his feet.

Nephi raises his head to look at Laman, but Laman won't return his stare. Instead, Laman turns toward me. His eyes are bloodshot from the seawater, and his face is pale and strained. He looks defeated, not recognizing this was a victory for his better self.

Nephi and I begin to pray, pleading for the storm to stop. The Liahona is in his hand. Laman and Lemuel just stand to the side watching the sea as our Savior does His work. Slowly the waves recede, gently the wind stills, softly the light grows. It is as if I am watching opposition retreat from the face of God.

There it is. The sun finally breaks through. Nephi looks up from the Liahona and half smiles at me. It must be working. Nephi leans against me and drops his head in relief.

Lemuel speaks first. "Nephi, I am sorry. I thought I was protecting us."

"Stubbornness will not stop God, but it will stop us." Nephi declares as he stands up on his own. "Someday soon, we will arrive at the land of promise, and you will know the Lord keeps His promises. Our sacrifices will be honored! On that day, we will build an altar and worship God for our deliverance. Laman, sacrifice your pride on that altar. Lemuel, sacrifice your fears. We must all sacrifice our sins. They are burdens that are only holding us back. Instead, feel hope in Christ!"

For days I have considered all the implications of that terrible storm. The Lord tutored me again in the critical lesson of opposition. As my father taught, there must be opposition in all things, but my sacrifices can be consecrated for my good. I must be learning because it brings a smile when it never has before. Have I not overcome opposition through Christ? Death is real, but I will live forever. My sins are blood red, but Christ washes them clean away. I am weak but can be strengthened by God. We were nearly lost at sea, but my family can never be lost to me. Are my sacrifices not worth these victories?

Victorious is God's greatest attribute. Yet only in opposition can we witness the Lord's victories. Do not be so eager for ease and comfort. They leave you unsteady, easily swept away by pride and wickedness. I needed hardship to recognize my sin. Opposition motivated me to sacrifice my pride with a broken heart and contrite spirit. Only then could I be empowered by the Savior who will overcome the world.

Christ is the perfect antidote to opposition because He is just and constant as opposition. If there were never a storm in life, how would I know what I am capable of? How would I learn what He is capable of doing for me? My sacrifices for the Lord make me strong. His sacrifices for me make me safe in a world I cannot control.

I had never seen an anchor so large until we molded one for this ship. God gave us this anchor, not for dead weight to carry across an ocean but as a solid assurance that it will someday anchor us in the promised land.

My covenants with God are my true anchor now. There is no longer anything I have not or would not give to my Lord. There is nothing good He has not or will not give to me. From one extremity of life to the next, I trust in my Lord. I know of a surety that He has consecrated my sacrifices and those of my family.

Sacrifice Is Always Worth the Effort

Was it reasonable for Christ to expect so much sacrifice from Nephi and his family? Is it reasonable for Christ to expect the most difficult sacrifices from you? Of course—because He always has something better in mind.

The reality is that God does not downgrade the faithful. Christ asked them to sacrifice what they thought was comfort and security in Jerusalem, only because He had something better in mind. Christ wanted Sariah to be the mother of a whole new civilization, not just another misguided neighbor captured by the Babylonians. He refined Lehi through his exceptional experiences to be an exceptional example, worthy of reverence that has lasted generations. Christ has something better in mind for you as well.

Laman was asked to sacrifice in the same way. In hindsight, can't you see how much better it would have been for him (and his posterity of millions) if he had consistently worked with Christ rather than against Him? If he had sacrificed his pride enough to obey, can you see how much hardship could have been avoided? His humility would have been worth the effort, especially given the ripple effects his choices had on generations of Lamanites and Nephites. Christ never imposed nor desired that much hardship to be part of his story. Laman created much of the hardship himself.

Connected with the law of sacrifice is the understanding that Christ will never downgrade you. Christ will always lead you toward something better, even if the journey requires great sacrifice and many years of waiting. Christ has even shown you the perfect example of how sacrifice works by the way He lived His own life.[9]

First, Jesus Christ focused on His goal (helping His family). He struggled, learned, and worked for us. He bowed His head, bent His knee, and bore our burdens, all for us. He stayed focused, even in death, on keeping *us* His main priority.

What did *He* gain from all His sacrifices? By working to create the world, Christ enabled both our physical births and His own. By bearing the cost of the Atonement, Christ ensured that families could be together forever and that He could be with His family. By submitting to the Crucifixion, Christ unlocked the Resurrection and eternal life for us, as well as for Him. Would Christ say that even the greatest sacrifice ever known was still worth the effort? Yes, I know He would.

Sacrifice requires taking a risk for righteousness while still trusting that you are not sabotaging yourself. This is not done blindly but rather with constant reassurance from the Holy Ghost, guidance from the prophet, and hope from covenantal promises. Christ does not expect you to continually gamble on whether faithful actions will eventually benefit you. He guarantees it by irrevocable decree through the law of sacrifice in the temple. We have thousands of years of history proving that sacrifice for righteousness is always worth it.

When the Israelites had completed their forty years of wandering (a.k.a. learning), they were finally faithful enough to possess "the ark of the covenant of the Lord of all the earth" (Joshua 3:11). They finally reached the border of their promised land. But the River Jordan was raging at flood stage, and they had to cross it.

Christ told the prophet Joshua that He would be magnified. Joshua humbly assured the people, "The living God is among you" (Joshua 3:10), and directed them to repent in preparation for a treacherous task. Joshua commanded them to follow the ark in order to "know the way by which [they] must go" (Joshua 3:4). In other words, no one would willingly walk into a raging river without the covenant power of Christ to assure them.

Following the prophet, while carrying the covenantal ark on their backs, twelve priesthood bearers passed through the camp. The people rose to follow. Reaching the river's edge, these men "dipped in the brim of the water" (Joshua 3:15), asserting their faith through action *before* witnessing a miracle. The river parted, the ark passed through on dry ground, and the people followed and "passed clean" into their promised land.

Following Christ's prophet while relying on their covenants was the only path that could have worked. And following *your* covenant path is the only way to get to *your* promised land.

The blessings Christ gives you will always be of greater value than the sacrifice we can give Him. We can only give in mortal, temporary ways. Christ gives back in permanent, eternal ways. In every book of scripture, and in the teachings of more than 150 prophets and teachers, we see the same pattern. Sacrifice is rewarded exponentially.

Prophet	The Sacrifice Made	The Blessings Received
Adam	- Had to leave the Garden of Eden - Learned to survive hardship and temptation - The first to lose a child to murder	- Became the father of humanity - Will lead the angelic hosts of heaven - Given the power to vanquish Satan
Enoch	- His people were threatened through violence - Taught a wicked group of people to be united	- Was given power to manipulate laws of physics - Translated directly to God's presence
Noah	- Believed God's revelation above all else - Resisted wickedness even when surrounded - Lived in isolation	- Rescued from the Flood - Taught many generations of his family - Like Adam, became father of the earth
Isaac	- Willingly submitted to his own human sacrifice, comparable to Christ	- Was promised worlds without number and eternal godliness by an angel
Moses	- Withstood Pharaoh's power - Wandered for forty years with the Israelites - Could not enter the promised land	- Became "one of the greatest of men" - Fed directly by God for forty years - Translated with Christ
Lehi	- Left his home and inheritance - Trekked through the desert - Sailed across an ocean to unknown lands	- Was protected from murder - Saw all the works of Christ in a dream - Successfully founded a new civilization
Alma	- Repented of his sins - Forgave his enemies, the Lamanites - Gave up his role as national leader	- Saw Christ surrounded by angels - Built a democracy; became chief judge - Led his son to repentance and salvation
Peter	- Left his livelihood as a fisherman - Crucified upside down	- Walked on water - Worked beside Christ for millennia
Moroni	- Protected the scriptures above all else - Lost his country and family - Spent many years in isolation	- Visited by the Three Nephites - Restored truth to his descendants - Became a herald of the Second Coming

Joseph Smith	- Lived honestly and humbly - Survived persecution - Repented after mistakes - Grieved for multiple family members - Murdered and falsely accused	- One of few to see God the Father - Translated new scripture from God - Restored Christ's priesthood power - Revealed the sealing of eternal families - Reestablished Christ's true Church

Let me give you one more example that is easier to measure.

How many times should you sacrifice your pride by forgiving someone else? Peter once asked this same question. You can read about it in Matthew 18:21–22.

$$70 \times 7 = 490 \text{ times!}$$

That is an incredibly high number. Forgiving the same person 490 times may seem almost ridiculous. After just the tenth time, I would probably revert to some immature name-calling and never talk to that person again.

But let's consider Christ's law of sacrifice. How many times has Christ forgiven you? Certainly, every time you repent. But how do we count that? We can't. But we can estimate how many times Christ offers you sanctification through the sacrament. If you counted every Sunday (except general conferences) from the age of two until one hundred, you would get:

$$(100–2) \times (52–2) = 4900$$

Therefore, Christ asks you to forgive 490 times, but He forgives you *at least* 4900 times.

$$490/4900 = 10\%$$

This means God is asking for no more than 10 percent of what He is offering to you. All without ever calling you names or abandoning you.

Might I suggest a very comforting exercise? Make a list of every promise God has made to you. I wish I could make a list for you of everything offered in the temple—it would be very long, with each line promising something grand. To imagine them all coming to pass makes my soul sing out to God, "How great Thou art!" The eternal life He offers is mountainously joyful and enduring. The goodness of these blessings is so massive that it far outweighs any possible righteous offering on your part. Making sacrifices for Christ will always be worth the effort because the blessings He gives you are exponentially better than what you can give Him.

How to Gain Christ's Power

A portion of power is granted to you every time you choose Christ's way over your other options. If Christ must follow the laws of justice, how is He able to be so generous with His blessings? Maybe His higher perspective gives Him a more accurate estimate of your eternal value. Maybe He knows you can grow to be exponentially more influential than you realize through your faithful sacrifices.

The abundance of opportunities He gives you to sacrifice is a genius way to help others while also ensuring He can bless us at the same time. Do you want further light, knowledge, ability, influence, strength, and power? You can gain all of that through your faithful and intentional actions to interact with Christ and the Holy Ghost. Here are a few examples:

Priesthood service	Church callings	Family service
Scripture study	Missions/missionary work	Community involvement
Building a family	Strengthening relationships	Bearing testimony
Fasting	Speaking in church	Diligence
Prayer	Tithing	Patriarchal blessings
Asking questions	Temple attendance	Journal writing
Come, Follow Me study	Humility	Keeping commandments
Word of Wisdom	Forgiveness	Repentance
Ministering	Education	Trusting Christ

These sacrifices are not a to-do list—they are an empowerment list! I'm grateful it's so long because there's a good fit for everyone on this list. Every day, you have a whole menu of empowerment options to choose from.

I'm sure you've heard it said that time is money. I think angels watching over us roll their eyes every time they hear a person say this.

Time is not money to God. Time is power! Christ is trying to direct you toward those efforts that will add to your eternal power.

By highlighting which efforts are the most valuable, Christ is maximizing your short mortal experience in the most effective way—by encouraging you to sacrifice what is easy for what is powerful.

All Shall Work Together for Your Good

It is in wisdom that the law of obedience and the law of sacrifice are presented together during the endowment ceremony. In Christ's gospel, you cannot have one without the other. Obedience without sacrifice has no ability to change you. Sacrifice without obedience has no authority to change you. For example, fasting for an hour doesn't require much sacrifice and doesn't mean much. But at the same time, fasting all day is just starving unless it is done obediently as He has asked and with a desire to honor God.

Doctrine and Covenants 98:3 teaches more about the blessings of sacrifice: "Therefore, he giveth this promise unto you, with an immutable covenant that they shall be fulfilled; and *all things* wherewith you have been afflicted *shall work together for your good*, and to my name's glory, saith the Lord" (emphasis added).

Adam and Eve made the covenant of the law of sacrifice shortly after leaving the Garden of Eden and entering the real world. Their covenants assured them that their hard work and self-reliance would "work together for [their] good." They chose to sacrifice certainty, beauty, and ease because the sacrifice allowed them to become parents and reach the celestial kingdom, granting them what they wanted most.

Remember, the Garden of Eden was not exaltation—it wasn't even heaven. By sacrificing the Garden of Eden, they gained access to something better than they already had. It was certainly hard, but exaltation was finally available to them through the "immutable covenant" of the law of sacrifice.

After His Crucifixion, Christ appeared in glory to the Nephites at the temple in Bountiful. He declared Himself as "the light and the life of the world" and "the God of Israel, and the God of the whole earth" (3 Nephi 11:11, 14). He also testified that the only reason He has this grand power is because He obeyed His Father's plan to be sacrificed "for the sins of the world" (verse 14). Even Christ's glory would be limited without His willingness to sacrifice.

Like Christ, your own empowerment will come through the sacrifices that Heavenly Father asks of you. Your temple covenants will make you Christ's disciple, even His apprentice. You will gain access to Christ's power precept upon precept, line upon line, as you consistently make faithful acts of sacrifice in the name of Jesus Christ and for the glory of your Heavenly Father.

The Value of Christ's Sacrifice

What do all your sacrifices add up to? What is the value of an obedient soul who is willing to sacrifice in God's honor? To be honest, I can't fully comprehend it. However, I do know what someone was willing to pay for it.

There is a law of economics, irrevocably decreed, that the value of anything depends on what someone is willing to pay for it. Jesus Christ paid for you with His life. To Him, you are worth the life of a God. To Heavenly Father, you are worth the life of a Beloved Son. It seems nearly impossible for me to imagine myself as so valuable. Yet this is not a purchase Christ regrets. He is not seeking to return you, or anyone else, for a full refund. Even the person with the lowest spiritual capacity can become like Christ by consistently applying His Atonement. Christ feels that His sacrifice was more than worth the effort. According to His own words, the worth of a soul is so great that if even one soul is saved by coming to Him in faithful repentance, then His joy is full (see Doctrine and Covenants 18:10–16).

Don't underestimate the value of daily, faithful sacrifices, even when effort is difficult and learning is slow. Your sacrifices are for a holy purpose. They increase your ability to become like your heavenly parents until you *are* a heavenly parent. Through sacrifice, Christ will teach you how to save souls.

Imagine a large hospital full of sick or injured people, with only one doctor to treat them all. The doctor certainly sacrificed years of effort and learning to gain the ability to help these people. With every life saved, there is joy. The sacrifice is worth it with every child, every soul, that is saved. Consider what would happen if one of these saved souls returned to the doctor and said, "Teach me so that I can work beside you. Teach me so that more lives can be saved." What would this training look like? How would it start? What would be required of the student? Once this student is fully trained, many more lives could be saved—just as many souls are saved as we live the law of sacrifice and participate in this grand work of salvation.

Chapter 5

The Law of the Gospel

Corianton

Alma's youngest son
Missionary to the Zoramites of Antionum
Returned home to Zarahemla
See Alma 39

My mission is not to be forgotten. It is where I learned of the reality of Jesus Christ. I had trodden the path toward true misery in Antionum, and the path toward true happiness became clearer. My true friends stepped forward, and the fault lines of my testimony were laid bare.

It took less than a year for me to go from the son of a prophet and missionary of Christ to one who had lost their faith and risked their virtue. It happened so fast. Anyone who thinks they're immune to such vulnerability does not fully understand their need for a Savior.

The seeds of my doubt were first planted as I sat in the back of a vast, hollow synagogue watching a pompous man, named Zoram, climb the narrow staircase of the Rameumptom. He was the self-appointed leader of the Zoramites. Dressed in his finest apparel, thronged by his loyal priests, he climbed his tower of arrogance. At the top, he edged his way onto the lonely platform to raise his hands high above his head and declare these words:

"Holy, holy God; we believe that thou art God. But we do not believe the childish traditions of our brethren. We believe thou has separated us from our brethren and elected us to be thy holy children; and also, Lord, thou hast made it known unto us that there shall be no Christ." (See Alma 31:12–23)

For what might have been the first time, I suddenly connected all the actions of past generations as a fight over one question: Either there is a Christ or there is not. But Zoram's speech inspired an idea that entered my mind like a warring Lamanite. Could there be a God without a Christ?

I loved God. I loved what He did for me. But could I have all the blessings of God without the warnings from Christ? Could I have exaltation without the need for redemption? Could I enjoy choices without laws—without punishments? My father was clearly heartbroken and frustrated that these people would work so unitedly toward a Christ-less effort. The implications of Christ *not* being real grew in my mind, but this idea did not bring forth good fruit.

The days went by unsuccessfully. They didn't respect my father, Alma, the former chief judge, founder of democracy, and prophet of Christ. They resented my princely companions—Aaron, Ammon, and Omner—for gifting the fertile lands of neighboring Jershon to the Anti-Nephi-Lehies. They kept their distance from Amulek and Zeezrom, knowing little about them. Zoram and his priests, however, were prosperous and compelling leaders. The people had no reason to seek guidance elsewhere.

Slowly but surely, my clarity, confidence, and self-control began to wane. I became more easily frustrated and impatient. When my father warned me that I knew the will of God and was therefore responsible for it, I lashed out at him.

Every day, Zoram would walk through town with a different woman on his arm, followed by his priests, to prove that consequences did not apply to him. Every day, he would overtly disrespect my father. It ate at my pride, having been among the elite and elect my whole life. How dare he!

I can look back on it and see where I went wrong. I wasn't humble. I wasn't working or teaching for Christ's sake. I wasn't even sure if Christ was real. But I knew that those who mocked us in the streets were real. I knew my embarrassment was real.

I came to fear ridicule more than I hoped for success as a missionary. I feared disrespect more than I hoped for power through Christ. My fearful lack of faith made me vulnerable to sin. I made sinful choices to avoid what I feared. These left me worse off than I started, sending me into a downward spiral of small missteps.

Then I met Isabel (see Alma 39:3–4). She made me feel confident again. For what felt like only a short time, I fell into her imaginary world where I didn't need Christ. I made bigger mistakes and was too prideful to deal with them.

Suddenly, I felt even more vulnerable than before. I needed the confidence she gave me more and more. That imaginary world with her was soft, warm, and carefree. I could pretend she was mine, even though she never said she would be. It wasn't real, but I convinced myself that this was what freedom and independence felt like.

I dropped my beliefs to the ground, and one day I thought to myself, "If we just left, we could stay this way." That last night felt like only one step further. Out in the woods, I lay with her, then held her in my arms, watching the stars above, pretending this imaginary world was all I would ever want.

It was then that I heard a crashing through the underbrush. Someone was coming fast through the trees. My brother Shiblon was yelling my name. "Cori! Cori, where are you?" He was scared. I sat up and called out. I heard him turn toward my voice, and I jumped up to go to him, but I stopped short.

Just beyond the firelight, Zoram and five of his priests were patiently watching us with greedy smiles on their faces. Shiblon came crashing through the trees seconds later, right into their arms.

He was terrified for me, but I had to watch his face as the realization of his own fate suddenly sank in. Shib was as trapped as I was. In that moment, in that split-second decision, I ran to Isabel. My loyal brother struggled against the priests, trying to save me and him, but I ran to protect her instead. I grabbed a half-burning log out of the fire and put my body between Isabel and Zoram.

I heard her reaction from behind me. "Stupid boy. You're nothing but bait."

She walked out from behind me and casually turned to walk away. I felt shocked and betrayed. Oh, how obvious this all was!

By the time I turned back to Shib, he was being held tightly by both arms. A priest wasted no time. He picked up a rock and knocked Shib out cold. I was left alone at the mercy of my father's enemies. My mind reeling, my heart pounding, it was only by a miracle that I heard a footstep behind me. Someone was there. With all my speed and strength, I swung the burning log behind me and to my right. I caught whoever it was off guard and grazed his face with embers. Crying in pain, he stepped to his left, blocking whoever was with him. I took my chance and sprinted for the trees, leaving my brother behind.

I raced toward my father's house, but I never made it. I was barely in town when a bright light and commotion caught my attention. A crowd had gathered in the square, agitated and angry. I heard my name in gruff, disgusted tones. There were people there who were followers of Zoram, but I also saw many of our friends whom we had taught.

A large, hooded figure grabbed my shoulders from behind while whispering my name. "Cori, come with me."

It was Amulek. He seemed to know what was going on, and I let him drag me into the shadows. He led me up an exterior staircase to a balcony above, and there we crouched against the far wall. From that vantage point, we could peer over the ledge and see the courtyard below.

"They know, Cori. Your father knows, everyone knows," Amulek said.

"What are you talking about? We have to get Shib. They have Shib." I struggled to get up again, but Amulek was much stronger.

"Shiblon… where is he? He was supposed to be with Omner."

"No! No, he's not. I was in the woods. I was with Isabel, and Zoram was there. He saw me. But Shib found me too. They have him, Amulek! We have to go back."

"Cori, wait! Listen to me. Zoram has been planning this for months. That crowd is gathered to watch Zoram expose your father as a heretic. He's been laying a trap for you from the beginning."

"*What?*" I reeled back and recalled what Isabel had said. Bait.

I shoved Amulek back against the wall and looked over the edge. There he was, my mighty father, surrounded by the crowd in the center of the square. His wrists and feet were chained to a post, but he stood tall and defiant. He spied me looking over the balcony above and lifted half a smile.

I felt faint. I felt helpless. I felt guilty.

Not long after, Zoram then entered the courtyard with his contingent of priests. Addressing the agitated crowd, he held his arms out wide.

"Thank you, my friends. You have come here at my bidding because in your hearts, you knew Alma the prophet was not trustworthy. It has not surprised you that he would be exposed as a liar of such grand claims. You are here because in your heart, you know I am right and have always been right."

Out of the crowd stepped Aaron, certainly no coward to empty threats.

"Charge him or release him, Zoram! Alma has never lied to these people. He has taught of Christ and denounced your hypocrisy. Your loyalties are to the Lamanites, not these people."

"Are the Lamanites so bad, Aaron? You call them brothers; you brought them home to us and even gifted them lands. Is it so bad that I wish to follow the example of your fellowship?"

"You should see the scars upon my back before you speak of loyalties and people you know so little about."

Zoram turned back to my father. "Perhaps you mean loyalties between a father and a son."

My heart sank, and my face went white. With a signal of Zoram's hand, Shiblon was brought forward, struggling against his captors (see Alma 38:3–5). They were going to accuse Shiblon publicly of adultery—in my place! They chained him to a post next to my father and doused him in cold water while he sputtered and gasped.

Standing next to Shiblon, Zoram addressed the crowd. "You have already heard the whispers of Alma's son Corianton, fraternizing with a harlot all around town. To add another shocking detail to the story, Shiblon was found this very night deep in the woods in the arms of the same harlot!"

The crowd erupted, clamoring for details in a frenzy of outrage. Clearly, Zoram had prepped them well.

"I have found him and brought him forward," Zoram continued, "not because I accuse him but because their own preaching condemns him. Is he truly a follower of this Messiah, or a lying hypocrite? Is his father a prophet of authority? If so, why can he not even control his own sons?"

Again, the crowd erupted in approval. Their calls for punishment were loudest of all. Turning to Shiblon, Zoram continued. "Under the law of Moses that you claim to honor, you know full well that the punishment for fornication is stoning. Was it not you we found in the woods, Shiblon?"

"I have faith and hope in Jesus Christ," Shiblon replied. "I believe in His word and honor His laws. He will judge those whom He will judge. I am at His mercy and gladly place myself at His feet. You have no power over me, Zoram!"

Zoram blustered till Shiblon cut him off, speaking directly to the crowd.

"You cannot stop people from learning of Christ!" The crowd responded with an angry cry.

"You will learn Zoram is a traitor!" Shiblon was purposely goading the crowd. The people clamored while Zorman tried to capture their attention again.

"You will all be punished for your sins!" Shiblon yelled out in defiance.

Finally, he challenged them, "Zoramites, take your aim!"

Those most agitated in the crowd took this as their cue. Zoram's control of the situation was overrun; the mock trial was too quickly discarded. Impulsively, the first stones began to fly.

From my rooftop, I gasped, "Shiblon, no!" *He was taking my stones!* Startled, Aaron, Ammon, Zeezrom, and Omner ran forward to stop them. My father pulled at his chains toward Shiblon. Even Zoram looked surprised and dismayed. He wanted the crowd to be fired up about my father, not flame out prematurely over Shiblon.

The stones were mostly aimed at Shiblon, but my father took his fair share—in the arms, in the chest, in the leg. At first, Shiblon tried to recoil and cower as best he could, but there was nowhere he could go. Crying out in pain, the stones came hard and fast. Our companions' efforts were blocking some throws, but they could not stop them all. My father was screaming and pleading for them to stop. Amulek's large arms pinned me to the wall, though I fought against him. I would have jumped from the balcony had I been free.

There was nothing I could do but watch my brother die in my place.

He was never supposed to be there. I never asked him to find me. How did he even know? The last few months were a snare laid for me by pride—not even Zoram's pride, but my own. I thought I didn't need a Christ. But in that desperate moment, I cried out in my loudest voice, "Christ! Save him!" I dropped my head against Amulek and yelled into his chest. "Save him!" Until that moment, I hadn't realized I needed Christ so much—or even that I loved Shiblon so deeply.

I watched Shib look to my father and say something. My father closed his eyes and held still. Slowly, Shiblon began to stand tall once again. A dozen stones flew past him, to the left and to the right. They flew too high or even bounced off the ground, but none hit his bruised and bloody body. Slowly, his countenance changed.

He quit flinching and shifting out of the way. The mood of the crowd changed. They must have thrown forty rocks by then and were running low, yet Shib was still standing true.

Mirroring Shiblon's stance, my father called out for all to hear: "Angels minister to the followers of Christ!" Catching his confidence, Shiblon called out as well: "Jesus Christ has given me strength!" (see Alma 31:33; Mosiah 24:14–15)

Unsatisfied, some in the crowd tried to force their way forward, but our companions held them back. With surprise in his voice, Shiblon testified, "Even this is swallowed up in my joy of Christ." (see Alma 31:38)

They still couldn't get to him. Sturdy and humble, he called out again. "He is the living God!" (see Alma 43:10)

Finally, the scales tipped. Those on the edges joined the struggle, pushing the agitators away. The crowd thinned, the tension dissipated, and the moment of fire and brimstone passed us by. Those who were at the front of the crowd looked for Zoram. Having lost the battle, he had already left unseen. Leaderless, the crowd began to disperse.

Amulek finally let me go, and I raced down the stairs.

We left Antionum the next day for the protection of Jershon without baptizing a single soul. I dreaded the ripple effects of my actions, having further enflamed the possibility of war. Clearly, I had the freedom to make choices, but I had no control over the consequences that followed.

Terrible shame and grief placed me in a chaotic state of mind. At one moment, I wanted to thrust the pain away as if I was manipulated into being faithless, denying my responsibility. In another instant, I feared I could never change, no matter what I did. Then my thoughts would shift again into panic over what would become of me and how I would be judged by people and by God. Part of me hoped Judgment Day would ever come.

I believe the Holy Ghost helped my father perceive the gaps in my understanding and how to fill them with Christ's true doctrine. He explained the reassurance I could feel when cradled in Christ's twin hands of justice and mercy. I see now that this peace is possible only through repentance (see Alma 12:32–35).

I feared not being good enough, so why try? I feared being faithful, just to find out I was a fool. Again, these fears made me vulnerable. I had to acknowledge how fear was at the root of my sins.

My father could also sense the unfairness in my heart. I felt entitled to something that I feared I would never receive, so I tried to get it my own way. In Antionum, my actions felt justified. I see now this was not the case. Christ is protecting me from the harm I bring upon myself and offers me joy in greater abundance than I can create on my own.

Is it fair to be held responsible for choices when you cannot foresee the consequences beforehand? I have come to understand that it's not a matter of fairness. My agency belonged to me even before I was a child of God (see Abraham 3:21–22; Doctrine and Covenants 93:29–31). He preserved my agency because God would not steal what was already mine, even if I use it unwisely. But He will teach me how to use it properly. I cannot deny His efforts to do so. I also cannot deny the warnings He and my father continually gave me beforehand. Still, I came so close to losing control of my soul. What would I have done without Christ?

I didn't have a complete understanding of the misery I could create, nor the misery Satan could create. Satan's influence can only make things worse. I should never have risked such a fate. Hearing of my father's vision while he was unconscious for three days has made so much more sense to me. It made me understand how much misery I was inviting and how much happiness I was pushing away. Why would I want to do such a thing?

Now I know I can be redeemed from even serious mistakes through repentance. It worked for my grandfather. It worked for my father. It will work for me.

Second Chances

Christ's promise of unconditional love can remove our feelings of vulnerability, leaving us less motivated to sin. Alma's teachings on restoration can help you feel more in control of your future (see Alma 41:12–15; Doctrine and Covenants 6:36). Your mortal actions do matter and do determine your eternal experience. It is within your control to be faithful, so it is within your control to be restored to a successful and happy state.

You no longer need to fear the disrespect that may come from others, the dissatisfaction life may bring, or the worry of missing out on opportunities. Yes, these feelings can come daily. But the love and blessings from our Savior can be a protective refuge from these feelings if you always remember Him (see Doctrine and Covenants 20:77–79). I love the refuge Christ offers me! He has opened a pathway to salvation, and I am choosing to walk with Him gratefully.

Corianton's experience brings a question to my mind: How is it fair for us all to be granted so many second chances because of one person's—even Christ's—Atonement?

This can only be the case if that one person's power is so pure, so far-reaching, and so valuable that to offer it as atonement outweighs all the pain, anger, hatred, and misunderstanding caused by our many ignorant sins. How honorable Christ must be! I have felt but a sliver of misery, which has swamped me, yet Christ's power must be so much greater. It is a love such as this that the gospel of Jesus Christ—even the plan of happiness—is built upon. There is no greater love than this.

Repentance is possible, but we must respect the awesome power of Christ. We must ponder the reality of it. We must want to be with Him. When you have a clear understanding of what you are choosing between, the choice becomes easier. Personally, I never want to live outside of Christ's influence. Christ's atoning power can return me to God. The closer I am to God, the happier I will be. Just as God is light, just as God is life, God truly *is* happiness (see Mormon 7:7).

The Promise of Love and Redemption

Corianton learned the critical role Christ plays in the plan of happiness. Indeed, he learned that our truest happiness is found only through the doctrine of Christ. As a temple covenant, the law of the gospel is your personal guarantee that Christ is the living Son of God and that His doctrine will lead to your happiness. It is His promise of love and redemption.

The doctrine of Christ is summarized within the law of the gospel. The endowment ordinance defines this as repentance, baptism by immersion for the remission of sins, receiving the gift of the Holy Ghost, engaging in ordinances, and enduring to the end. Notice how receiving temple ordinances is included as a necessary step of exaltation.

The law of the gospel requires you to respect commandments, especially the two most important: to love God with all your heart and to love your neighbor as yourself. All other commandments are necessary because we aren't great at recognizing when we're wandering off track from the first two commandments, especially in areas of materialism, sexual sin, and pride. Corianton did not foresee the ripple effects of his actions, and often neither can we.

Even if we recognize Christ through obedience and gain His power through sacrifice, we are still prone to commit sin. This sin separates us from God and dampens our ability to receive His power. The law of the gospel promises that you can be cleansed from sin and retain your closeness with God through the Atonement of Jesus Christ. It is the promise that your mortal practice period will not derail your eternity.

To keep the law of the gospel, you must develop a deep respect and understanding for the Atonement of Jesus Christ. In other words, you are covenanting to repent frequently, even daily. You are acknowledging that repentance is necessary to retain the power you have already been granted and remain safe from Satan's corruption.

Let Christ Have Full Sway in Your Heart

Alma the Younger taught Corianton to "let the justice of God, and his mercy, and his long-suffering have full sway in your heart" (Alma 42:30). I ask you to carefully study Alma's teachings to his sons (found in Alma 36–42). Alma is teaching the law of the gospel from a higher perspective and broader context than nearly any other prophet. He is one of the few authorized to describe the full misery of Satan versus the full happiness of Christ. His testimony should be taken very seriously. The redemption of Christ rescued him from the "eternal torment" of the "pains of a damned soul" to the "marvelous light" of full joy that was "so exquisite and sweet" (see Alma 36:6–23).

Alma emphasized the role of mercy and justice to help Corianton understand the contrast between the love of Jesus Christ and the misery of Satan. Alma explains *why* we should willingly follow Christ toward redemption. Think of misery and happiness on a scale from left to right. Mercy and justice set the rules for how we navigate the spectrum.

Christ's Mercy, Part 1: Justice will be answered, for there is no victim-less sin. However, Christ's mercy has created a grace period, temporarily delaying the justified punishment while you learn and, hopefully, seek repentance. With long-suffering patience, Christ is shielding you from most of what Satan could do. This first protective power of mercy is granted by God, enforced by Christ, and described in the temple as "enmity" between us and Satan (see Moses 4:21; Genesis 3:15, including chapter heading).[10] Christ is fighting this tremendous fight, keeping Satan's powers at bay, because He loves you. Satan does not have full access on earth—not yet. Figuratively speaking, he can only bruise your heel rather than crush your head.

Christ's Mercy, Part 2: The Atonement of Jesus Christ is a second great act of mercy. Christ offers you the option of repentance, a key to escape through the barrier of justice (if you choose it). Gratitude should fill your heart as Christ prompts you to try again.

Law of Justice, Part 1: The law of justice also acknowledges our sins, ensuring our separation from Christ until we sincerely repent. You choose your own eternity several times a day with every sinful or faithful choice. Judgment Day will be an acknowledgment of who you have become.

Law of Justice, Part 2: The law of justice is the perfect counterbalance to the law of mercy. The law of justice allows the use of a different key. This key of pride will give anyone the ability to unleash their punishment by willingly choosing Satan over Christ.

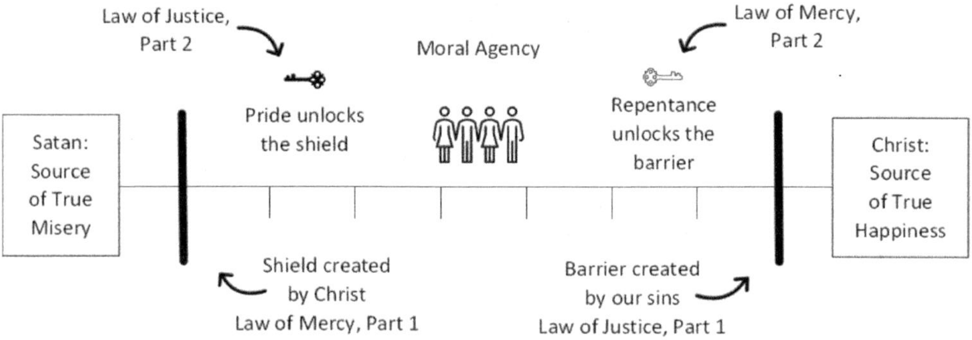

Our mortal definitions of misery and happiness are incomplete because none of us has experienced the ends of the spectrum. Since I have never been with Satan, I cannot comprehend the great depths of horror that are possible. As painful as even your worst memory could be, it would certainly be worse if Satan were unbound (see Doctrine and Covenants 76:43–48). On the opposite end of the spectrum, you and I have also not yet experienced the true heights of happiness that are possible with Christ. Your happiest memory is also just a taste of what it's like to be with God (see Isaiah 60).

Please remember the necessary symmetry between the law of mercy and the law of justice. Do not plead for Christ to be more present in our temporal world than He already is until the appointed time. If Christ were more present, then Satan would have to be more present, as well. Otherwise, the fairness of our test would be off balance. None of us would want this outcome. So instead, we must choose to move ever closer to Christ. The law of the gospel is a promise that we can indeed come to Christ.

Since our focus is short and our understanding incomplete, this mortal experience helps us experience part of the spectrum between sinfulness and misery versus righteousness and happiness. We learn firsthand the foundational truth that repentance brings happiness, while wickedness never does (see Alma 41:10). The merciful Atonement of Jesus Christ makes this possible. The law of the gospel is the promise that Christ can save you.

Corianton temporarily disregarded his precarious position and his need for saving. Perhaps he assumed that even if punishment was real, he could handle the cost of his sin on his own. This false theory should not be trusted. Corianton also confused his time with Isabel as happiness, but he learned it was only a dim counterfeit. Alma's testimony corrected Corianton's perception of how miserable payment could be and how joyful redemption would be.

Love for Repentance

It's not uncommon for a typical person to react so dramatically to correction that it mirrors a fight-or-flight response. Alma the Elder learned from Abinadi how prideful people typically react when their sins are pointed out (see Mosiah 12–13).

Choices	Reaction	Outward Expressions
Situation #1	Get angry, be easily offended	"What did you just say?" "Why are you lying about me?"
Situation #2	Discredit, spread misinformation	"Who are you to tell me what to do?" "You don't really care about me."
Situation #3	Deny there's a problem, rationalize	"It's not even a big deal." "There's nothing wrong with it."
Situation #4	Disregard the relationship, avoidance	"Just leave me alone." "Stop talking to me."
Situation #5	The worst option—deny Christ is needed	"I can take care of myself." "Nothing bad is going to happen."

Keeping the law of the gospel means trying your very best not to react in any of these ways, especially toward God. Instead, take a deep breath and remember that it's okay to make mistakes. Repentance is a holy thing, even an opportunity to become a little bit more like God.

It is so tough to admit when we have done something wrong. God knows how we mortals struggle to change our hearts sincerely. This is where His two-way covenant of the law of the gospel comes into play. It takes the sting out of vulnerability. It will stabilize you through missteps, comfort you with grace, and guide you to the answers that are always right. We change more easily when we feel safe.

The law of the gospel reassures us of two truths: You will always be loved (even in your mistakes), and you can always be good enough to get what you want. This covenant solidifies in a contractual form something you should already know. The ordinance gives you a vivid memory of when God personally promises His love, not just generally. Now you have more to rely on when you question His commitment to you. It creates the environment necessary to make repentance easier for our stubborn hearts.

You Will Always Be Loved

One of the great fears of all God's children is that we are not loved or accepted. Satan authored shame, and he uses this lie effectively. Shame triggers fears of judgment, abandonment, loneliness, and disrespect. These fears are real and deeply embedded in our survival instincts. God knows this and answers our fears through irrevocable covenant—solid ground, firm foundation, the rock of our Redeemer. The gospel of Jesus Christ was given out of love, the Atonement was completed out of love, and the relentlessness of our Heavenly Father to care for us is an act of love.

I am sure it was a comfort to Corianton to hear about his father's and his grandfather's experiences. Both were stalwart prophets who first sought repentance from deep sins. Knowing these men personally, he was able to see up close the progress possible in the human heart. The miracles of their forgiveness are meant to support us as well.

Your Heavenly Father knows that you will *do* better when you *know* better. He loves you and is graciously patient as he tries to fill in the gaps in your understanding. Therefore, you could betray your family and still be loved. You could wreck a stolen car and still be loved. You could burn the scriptures and still be loved. You could punch your sarcastic friend in the nose and still be loved. You get the idea. You cannot progress while doing those things, but you can still be loved.

Jesus Christ will not remove the mortal ripple effects of sin (so don't do any of the things I just mentioned!), but He *can* save you from the spiritual trap of sin. The law of the gospel guarantees that His love will be constant. The law of the gospel is in effect strong enough to save you even from yourself—if you follow Christ's directions.

You Will Always Be Good Enough

Another deep fear for most humans is not being good enough. This is a fear of failure, ridicule, letting someone down, or not reaching our potential. Interestingly, most people fear being last more than they hope to be first. These fears manifest themselves in an obsession with wasted effort, lost time, having the most, being better than others, or being selfish with material possessions. It can also create a self-imposed roadblock, where you refuse to put effort into what seems like a hopeless cause.

Too often, we believe that our goals, aspirations, and desires are lost because we're weak or hindered in some way. The law of the gospel flips this untruth on its head. If you remain partnered with Christ, high hopes can be preserved. Progress gained will not be lost because of mistakes. You can continue forward. Your promised success is always achievable because you have access to a deep well of ability through Christ's grace.

Wicked success will always be inferior to faithful defeat because the law of the gospel can shift defeat into a temporary condition. The only factors are faith, repentance, and time. All vain pursuits will crumble, while all virtuous efforts will progress for eternity. Eternity is what you have, for you will be immortal through the Resurrection of Jesus Christ. The more you work on eternal efforts, the happier you will be.

Importantly, progress can be made. Your effort to read your scriptures can make you progressively wiser. Your effort to pay tithing can make you progressively selfless. Your effort to apologize can make you progressively humbler. Your effort to attend the temple can make you progressively resilient. Your efforts to learn can make you progressively skillful. This happens because the gospel of Jesus Christ is based on making progress. You can always be good enough, because progress, paired with hope in Christ, will lead to success. Be careful not to disparage the faith-promoting progress you have already made. Do not act as if your faithful efforts are too small to be seen and magnified by Christ.

In the temple video, I particularly love watching the expressions on Adam and Eve's faces as they are taught about the Atonement—this lifeline to all they desire: progress, family, and living in God's presence. They no longer must stay in the garden; they no longer need to choose between God and family. They thought partaking of the fruit would make them not "good enough," but the Atonement of Jesus Christ allowed them to have a family and retain their promised return to God. Because of Christ, they could still be good enough to get everything most important to them, without compromise. As they continually rededicated themselves to their covenants and repented of their mistakes, no blessing of God could be withheld from them.

You can make mortal mistakes and still retain your promised return to God through the law of the gospel. Christ's power enables you to make continual progress toward what is most important to you. You can always be good enough to receive all of God's blessings through your faithfulness in Christ.

How to Keep Christ's Power

Christ's power cannot be kept in an unholy vessel for very long. The law of the gospel provides you a way to retain Christ's power and preserve your progress—even as you struggle through your next steps—if you repent of your mistakes frequently along the way. If you don't, your blessings, abilities, and protections can begin to rust. The length of time between your sin and your repentance is an important factor. *Daily* repentance retains your power quite effectively—while *yearly* repentance does so less.

You'll read about the mighty warrior-prophet Mormon in the next chapter. This superhero didn't have any superpowers that you or I don't have. Although he was surrounded by sin and destruction for most of his life, he remained uncorrupted because he consistently repented. As President Russell M. Nelson stated, "Daily repentance is the pathway to purity, and purity brings power."[11]

Joseph Smith offers us a modern example of this principle. Trying to be the prophet Christ needed him to be, with no modern precedent of what that looked like, would have been very difficult. Allowing Martin Harris to take the first 116 pages of the Book of Mormon transcript was a mistake Joseph, I'm sure, wishes he could take back (see Doctrine and Covenants 3, section heading; 10, section heading). Joseph had struggled and sacrificed deeply for those pages. They were tangible evidence of his priesthood gifts and spiritual progress. They were as sacred to him as my covenants are sacred to me.

When serious sin is committed, the fear of losing your covenant promises is very real. When the pages were lost, Joseph feared his priesthood gifts and revelatory progress would be lost forever. It was in this deep moment of despair that the law of the gospel was so necessary. For a time, Joseph's power to translate and his ability to receive revelation were hindered. But as he repented, Christ restored the powers Joseph once used. Joseph learned critical lessons through the experience, which refined his understanding of his special relationship with God. With time, he became the prophet we needed him to be.

Christ once again displayed His mind-blowing problem-solving power by preparing for Joseph's mistake 2,400 years earlier. Nephi was directed to write a summary of Lehi's record, and Mormon was directed to preserve both records (see Words of Mormon 1:3–7). Thus, Joseph later translated the prophecies we needed. The progress already made was not lost after all.

Our souls can also remain worthy of spiritual gifts. Because of Christ's problem-solving power, you don't need to start over at the beginning every time you sin. The guarantee is that through frequent repentance, the sacrament, and, if necessary, counseling with your bishop, even the great blessings of the temple will not be lost to you permanently. Your peace and enjoyment in the gospel can be retained.

Your repentance process will help you better understand how much Christ understands you. Repentance will help you better visualize how Christ can make you into a person of divine success, far exceeding your expectations. The Atonement allows you the chance to dust yourself off and try again.

I hope Joseph's example helps you feel less anxious about your ability to keep temple covenants for the rest of your life. Christ has promised you immortality, redemption, and exaltation. I have detailed Joseph's story to show you how these miraculous blessings are possible if given enough time. Repentance, paired with Christ's grace, will give you the endurance and capability to see your holy work through to the end.

Many people wait to receive their endowment because they want to delay the amount of time they are under covenant obligation. Choosing when to receive your endowment is a very personal, spiritual process led by the Holy Ghost in conjunction with counseling with your bishop. Take the time you need to decide for yourself when the time is right for you. But please understand—your covenants are steps on the ladder of success, not roadblocks.

Chapter 6

The Law of Chastity

Mormon

General of the Nephite armies
Awaiting battle in the Land of Joshua
See Mormon 1–2

My name is Mormon. I was named after my father, a man of foresight and action. He saw the corruption of sin within our enemies and within our own borders. After 200 years of blessed peace, our judgments, hearts, and homes have slowly succumbed to vanity, immorality, and pride. I have met these three deadly threats in all parts of my nation.

But it didn't have to be this way! Needless waste. Unending dissatisfaction. The Light of Christ was there—so available and abundant! But we threw it all away. For what? Day after day of bloodshed and contention. Night after night of empty lust and abuse.

As I camp on this battlefield, dreading what will yet again be great destruction, it is the vast wastefulness that stirs my anger. My soldiers have been fighting for their freedom on the battlefield by day while entrapping themselves in sin by night. Military victories mean little when wickedness ensnares them in a cycle of distraction, weakness, and incompetence.

They cannot follow directions because they're obsessed with avoiding any sacrifice it might require. They cannot trust me because they don't know how it feels to be trustworthy. They don't believe I can help them because their own misguided efforts have never led to satisfaction. They cannot hold firm because they have never developed relationships deep enough to be worth the fight. They have lost hope because their obsession with personal gain has led to loneliness. They destroy themselves and don't even see it!

I consider myself young because I know of those who came before me—men and women of valor, morality, and capacity who once held firmly to the ideals of righteousness and Nephite culture. I have been general of the mighty Nephite forces since I was a boy of just sixteen. It's strange to feel so young yet be so revered by my people. I am grateful to be a source of direction, but I do not feel honored by it. It is a sign of decay within the Nephite legacy.

They have called me to be their general because they're incapable of the focus and dedication required to do it themselves. Where are those of age who should be my superiors? They are either gone or proven to have a smaller portion of my wisdom.

Countless times have I witnessed the disease of wickedness and strife pollute the hearts of those around me. Such utter disloyalty to God. Such disdain for wholesome morality. Even a complete disregard for family responsibilities. Boys who should have been my friends have grown deeply selfish, almost as if happiness were a finite resource to be stolen from others to hoard for oneself.

I will not turn my back on the true source of strength: My Redeemer and Teacher, even Jesus Christ. Because of my virtue, God has given me tools to stem the flood of corruption and immorality that threatened to overwhelm me. He has granted me the gift of discernment to peer into the hearts of those around me. I have the gift of daily repentance, cleansing me of the tremendous pressure to break my fidelity. I have the clarity of mind necessary to see examples all around me of where I would be without the atoning grace of Christ.

When I was alone, Christ also gave me mentors and friends through the words of past prophets: Nephi, Mosiah, Alma, Ammon, Helaman, and Moroni. As I have read their writings over and over again, these men have become my exemplars and stalwart friends.

Their stories have become life-size in my mind, almost as if I were serving Christ alongside them. Through deep spiritual experiences, I have been with them all. I sailed on Nephi's ship, I declared my faith at King Benjamin's tower, and I ministered to Ammon's Lamanites. Currently surrounded by feckless soldiers, all I really want is to be among my 2,000 stripling brothers again.

I have scoured three cartloads of holy writing—words of might and strength and power like nowhere else. Without exception, every sanctified voice testifies that the direction of Christ works! His covenants are the only real power on earth.

As a reader, writer, prophet, and historian, I recognize the importance of being spiritually loyal to God. I know from experience that aligning your mind and soul to His direction increases your mind and soul beyond its current bounds.

But I am also a commander of many wicked men. I charge into battle; I break bones, and I kill those who would kill me. I therefore understand the reasons for being physically loyal to God all too well. I understand the gravity of harnessing your desires and energies for God's purposes and ambitions, lest you be lost in reactionary and even self-defeating behaviors. True loyalty requires mind, soul, *and* body. Otherwise, it is a false loyalty, held at arm's length in times of difficulty. If I depend on physical blessings, I must offer physical loyalty. Only then do I align with my purpose and potential.

My virtue has always been my strength in difficulty because my Savior increases my abilities when I am worthy of His help. He gave me added stature when I was small, added wisdom when I was naive, added soberness when I was distracted, added opportunities when I was obscure, added insight when I was unsure, and added stamina when I was exhausted. None of this could have been possible if I were only partly loyal to God. My chastity has been the bridge to my success, holding me up above the filth that would bring me down.

Now, in the faces of my wife and infant son, I can see goodness again. By the hand of my Lord, He is creating my family for a higher purpose. Human creation does not begin and end with a sexual act. Creation is a process that continues throughout our eternal lives. As we remain chaste and loyal to God, our divine creation will continue to lead to greater and greater ends.

My hope is not to hinder my Savior's creative process. "Create me still!" is my constant prayer. "Make me in thine image as I grow into a son of God. Empower me as I hold fast to the morals thou hast taught me."

I yearn for my family, and yet they are perpetually far away. Only Christ knows how to calm my heart. Only Christ knows what to say when I cry for them on the eve of battle. I believe He has a plan for us to be together.

Few listen to my teachings as a spiritual leader. At times, I feel entirely alone in my beliefs. Will only my family benefit from my faith? I don't see any other outcome, but I also know of Christ's miracles. His gospel will not be lost; I don't yet know exactly how He will do it. I just know that today I love my Savior, and that is enough for now.

I have been deemed the best the Nephite nation can produce, but I am not of their making. The hands of my Savior have increased me in strength, intellect, foresight, and diligence according to His goodness and my loyalty. Therefore, my complete devotion belongs to my Savior and my family until my dying day. Only the hand of Christ can shepherd me now.

Chastity Increases Capability

Chastity increases your capability.

I would repeat this phrase 100 times if it meant you would remember it. It has been illustrated and proven through every book of scripture. Chastity is such a sensitive topic that images of hermits, nuns, fire, or brimstone seem to be evoked whenever it is brought up. People can sometimes close themselves off to open discussion, missing out on the blessings promised. Often overlooked is that chastity brings an enhanced joy, not a tightly regulated joy. Chastity is not just a physical commandment (see Doctrine and Covenants 29:34–35). Chastity is not just about the sexual or physical things you should *not* do; the law of chastity is also about the *many* things, both physical and spiritual, you will be *better able* to do by following it. The law of chastity is empowering and hopeful, not judgmental or harsh.

As the fourth covenant, the law of chastity builds on the blessings from the previous three. You're asked to commit to chastity only after being told that your test will be fair, you will be generously rewarded, and you are loved. With the law of chastity, you are promised that you can be more than you imagined. As you align your life with the doctrine of Christ—to the point that you're seeking moral cleanliness to honor Him—then you cannot help but become more like Him. Becoming like Christ will always increase your personal capability.

Let's start with Mormon, an example of one of the most capable men ever to live.

It would be difficult to name anyone in known human history as capable as Mormon. He was spiritually confirmed as a prophet of God at the age of 15 (see Mormon 1:15). He was appointed as the leader of the sizable Nephite military by the age of sixteen. Later in life, he compiled the Book of Mormon by condensing a massive amount of scripture, an act that required great intelligence, deep spiritual insight, and sustained fortitude. That one success alone will change the world until the last generation.

Mormon must have held a comprehensive understanding of self-mastery, management, strategy, science, politics, law, culture, history, literature, and theology. However, he also deserves credit as the father and mentor of Moroni, who was a prophet and possessed the unique stamina needed to become the protector of the gold plates and the herald of the Second Coming of Jesus Christ. Beyond this, Mormon (and his son) witnessed the annihilation of the Nephites—hundreds of thousands of dead—yet remained faithful and hopeful until their dying day.

There is no doubt that Mormon had power beyond human capacity. It didn't come by chance; Mormon chose to repent daily and remain morally clean throughout his life despite being surrounded by those who did not (see Moroni 9:3–6). Mormon's soberness was recognizable because he understood the power of self-control and loyalty over selfishness and indulgence.

Mormon's capacity was increased powerfully, not *in addition* to being chaste, but *because* he was chaste. As Mormon's government position forced him to grow up, he found that no amount of money, education, status, or influence would bring him the success he wanted. He could get no further than he already was without Christ's partnership.

Mormon was loyal to himself, his future wife and child, and most importantly, to Christ. He did not hold back any part of his dedication. Instead, he gave all of it to God in complete fidelity. Physically, spiritually, intellectually, and emotionally, his soul was unified in reliance on and hope in Christ.

Christ is offering you an "invigorating future," as President Nelson taught, one that is partially predicated on the law of chastity. He is not offering you a consolation prize. He is not offering a gift you will never use again or that doesn't fit well. He is offering to fulfill your greatest joys forever.

When you were in the premortal world, you passed your first test by choosing to follow Heavenly Father's plan. This was called "keeping your first estate," which opened the way for your next step: being born on earth with a physical body. Now your second test is whether your physical self can *also* commit to Heavenly Father's plan. This is referred to as "keeping your second estate." Keeping your second estate opens the next step in your progress toward an exalted body and its exalted abilities.

As a spirit, you have already committed to Christ. You have already learned and loved the whole plan, but now your spirit is within your physical body. When you physically act against your spiritual potential, you create conflict within your own soul. In contrast, when you work together toward a righteous intention, you increase in strength, stamina, and momentum. I can feel this effect while I am in the temple, and it stays with me long after I have left.

It is while you are chaste that you demonstrate to Christ your full commitment to keep your second estate. You must govern some of your most instinctive physical impulses. Because of the empathy gained through the Atonement, Christ perfectly understands how chastity might impact you personally. He does not want you to pretend that these instincts don't exist; rather, He wants you to trust that following His commandments, by being an agent unto yourself (see Doctrine and Covenants 58:28), will increase your abilities.

How to Increase in Christ's Power

Again, the law of chastity is not just about all the sexual things you should not do. It is equally about what you will be better able to do because of your loyalty to Christ.

There are many all-consuming pursuits people seek in this world, such as strength, influence, wealth, knowledge, pleasure, and companionship. Unfortunately, chastity does not tend to rank very high on people's priority lists. In our modern day, a *lack* of chastity is often brandished as a badge of honor. Instead, think of chastity as a covenant superpower. Chastity is a deciding factor in whether Christ will grant you all other powers in the long-term.

To see some real-life examples of this, let's look at how Christ has highlighted chastity in the scriptures.

Samson: The Strongest Man to Ever Live

Samson's strength was unparalleled to the extent that he killed 1,000 men with nothing but a bone. He brought down a palace with only his two bare hands.

How did Samson lose his strength? It wasn't through cutting his hair—that was only an outward symbol of his covenant relationship. His downfall began with breaking the law of chastity through an affair with Delilah, who ultimately betrayed him (see Judges 13–16).

King David: The Most Influential Man

Who doesn't know the story of David and Goliath? Most people from various cultures are familiar with the story. Sports fans, businesspeople, and children on the street know the story and are inspired by it. It's been estimated that the story of young David slaying the mighty Goliath with only a rock and a sling is among the most widely known in the world. After Goliath, David went on to unite his country and command the respect of world powers.

How did David lose his status? He broke the law of chastity by initiating an extramarital affair with Bathsheba (see 2 Samuel 11–12; Doctrine and Covenants 132:38–39).

King Solomon: The Wealthiest and Wisest Man to Ever Live

Based on current estimates, Solomon's net worth would be $2.1 *trillion* in today's dollars. That is almost 500 percent more than Elon Musk and Jeff Bezos combined. Not only that, but Christ promised Solomon that no one before or after him would ever be as wise. As if these blessings were not enough, Christ even added longevity to the list, just for good measure. Solomon could enjoy these extreme blessings if he walked in Christ's way and obeyed His commandments.

How did Solomon lose such God-like blessings? His downfall started with breaking the law of chastity by marrying women Christ told him not to lust after (see 1 Kings 3–4, 11).

These are a few prominent examples of how a lack of chastity can be a handicap. The Lord has also given us prime examples of chastity being used properly as a catalyst for success. Mormon was one example; President Nelson was another.

President Nelson: The Most Powerful Man on Earth

President Russell M. Nelson would have very little of the respect and recognition he has today if he had made morally unclean choices. He led Christ's Church in the latter days as a seer and revelator. He held the keys of Christ's priesthood power on earth. His greatest joy expands with each additional member of his large family. Additionally, during his time as a doctor, President Nelson was inspired by God regarding the heart-lung machine, which was in its early stages of development. He also perfected many surgical heart procedures. This is remarkable when you consider that heart disease is the leading killer of humans globally. Tens of *millions* of lives have been saved by these technologies and procedures.

President Nelson attributed his most impressive successes to divine guidance and the companionship of his wife. When he passed, he retained great fortunes of compassion, intelligence, wisdom, talent, memory, and satisfaction. Each of these accomplishments could have been greatly hindered or lost completely without moral loyalty to God.

In each prior example, chastity was mandatory in retaining or enhancing all other abilities. Strength, influence, wisdom, wealth, power—they mean nothing if you cannot keep them. Christ has shown that only He can increase these powers well beyond human capacity or even human rationality. As you keep the law of chastity, Christ will improve and preserve your powers beyond what they could be otherwise.

By engaging in casual sex, you risk distraction, heartache, bitterness, illness, selfishness, and a whole host of unintended outcomes, including lost opportunities for something better. Over time, immorality can lead to a profound sense of disconnection and numbness. These hardships and their ripple effects are self-inflicted and avoidable. Even sex isn't enough to make it feel better because sex without commitment will never replace true belonging, partnership, and security.

In some cases, another person's choice to break the law of chastity can have a harmful effect on you or your family. This can result in some of the most difficult human experiences. Christ knows this and teaches the law of chastity to prevent it. His Atonement is the best help for the hardship caused by immorality because it is the ultimate source of belonging, partnership, and security.

This might sound a little surprising, but I felt my greatest happiness during each of my daughters' baby blessings. In those moments, my belonging, partnership, and security felt very real. The babies I loved most were safe, secure, and happy. I had a partner proving he was as committed to my goals as I was. We were worthy of receiving God's miracles on behalf of my daughters. This fulfilling purpose, sincere connectedness, and divine help combined to make me the happiest I had ever been. Because of our chastity, we could accomplish what we wanted most.

You don't need to choose between God and what you want most. If you dig deep enough, you can usually find a righteous desire at the root of a sinful one. Often, we try to fulfill our righteous desires in the wrong way. Perhaps your desire is belonging, partnership, security, or love. Through righteous covenant, God will help you get what you ultimately want in the best, most lasting way, not in an ineffective or sinful way. Stumbling blocks arise when you pursue these powers in a way contrary to what Christ has asked you to do. If He leads you away from a relationship that is not right for you, or warns you that pornography is wrong, or teaches you to keep your thoughts and actions clean, or to follow the prophet's warnings, it's not because He wants to deny you what you want. He just knows that what you're doing is jeopardizing what you want most.

CHASTITY BRINGS LIVING WATER

Early in Christ's earthly ministry, before revealing himself openly as the Son of God, Christ traveled to the Samaritan town of Sychar, part of the ancient birthright of the tribe of Ephraim. This town was also home to Jacob's Well, a revered spring dug by Israel, the father of the twelve tribes, and his sons. Despite being situated on a hilltop, the well had never run dry in almost 2,000 years.

In a way that felt quite purposeful, Christ met a woman at this much-needed well on a sweltering day and spoke with her alone (see John 4). But she wasn't just any woman—she was a woman breaking the law of chastity.

Christ asked her for water—a simple request—but she responded with disdain. Why would an Israelite want to talk to her, a Samaritan? Based on centuries of deep animosity between these two peoples, she expected to find judgment in His face, but it wasn't there. This surprised her.

Again, He asked for water. Again, she rebuffed Him. Despite this, He offered her something of supreme value in that barren land—water that would never run dry. Standing at the famous, beloved, dependable, even holy well of Father Jacob, the woman was unconvinced that such a miracle could occur twice. Such an offer could only come from the Messiah. It took a minute, but she began to realize that it had.

Christ then offered something even greater than living water. She could have within her "a well of water springing up into everlasting life" (John 4:14). He offered to make her into a symbolic fountain of living water. In other words, He offered to make *her* into a freely flowing, purely clean nourisher of souls, quencher of discomfort, and giver of life. He offered her some of the abilities He has Himself.

Astonished, she asked how it was to be done, desiring this for herself. Seemingly out of context, Christ then immediately directed her to come to Him with her husband, though He knew full well that the man she was living with was not her husband. Suddenly, she knew that He knew the moral mistakes of her past and present. It was a miracle she did not recoil defensively. What was it that overcame this common human reflex?

Again, He declared His authority as the Son of God. Again, He declared His ability to make her into what she valued most. But He made it clear that this transformation could not move forward without honoring the law of chastity (see John 4:16–18). Despite Christ's life-altering critique, this woman must have felt His love so deeply that she does not reject Him—she rejoiced! Full of hope, she ran into the city, becoming the first missionary allowed to openly declare the living Son of God.

This is the first instance I know of the living Christ teaching the law of chastity. Notice how He begins by teaching what is possible through chastity, no less than becoming a source of power like unto Christ. He doesn't compromise the sexual boundaries that God has set, but He first emphasizes how valuable chastity can be.

Unrepentant sins of immorality will stop the promises of greater power. In contrast, if your actions have been forgiven through the Atonement and you are fully loyal to Jesus Christ, He will symbolically make you into a well of living water, including giving you the power to heal, nourish, comfort, clean, and grow.

Jacob's Well still holds water to this day, another 2,000 years later. You can visit this well and know for a fact that you are standing within feet of where the Savior once taught the covenant of chastity and the incredible promise of power tied to it. Thousands more years can pass away, yet His promise of increased power will never run dry.

The Wise Order of Covenants

This is a good time to point out the great wisdom of the covenant order, because the law of chastity is so personal that it tends to trigger lots of vulnerabilities, which bubble to the surface in the form of "what if" questions. Usually, there is a fear at the root of each question:

What if it's too tempting? (The fear of difficulty.)

What if virtue doesn't matter that much? (The fear of wasted effort.)

What if I never love someone like this again? (The fear of lost opportunity or happiness.)

What if they leave me? (The fear of loneliness.)

These "what if" questions are so important. There are many others we could add. But don't let these fears distract you from the comfort God is trying to offer. Remember each covenant and what blessing is offered in return. Can you see how your underlying fears are addressed even *before* chastity is asked of you?

Covenant	**Promised Blessing**	**Comforted Fear**
Obedience	Freedom, customized fairness, and support	Oppression, betrayal, too difficult
Sacrifice	Your efforts will be well rewarded	Wasted time or effort, lost opportunity
The Gospel	You are loved and good enough	Loneliness, being last
Chastity	Increased capability	Mediocrity, lack of success
Consecration	All that the Lord has, joyful fulfillment	Worthlessness, unhappiness, loss

Can you see how covenants build on each other to create an environment where spiritual confidence can thrive? Before being asked to remain morally clean, you are first offered the guarantees necessary to calm your fears about being morally clean. Even better, after committing to chastity, you are promised every possible blessing to increase your motivation.

The topic of chastity becomes heated because it impacts so many human needs. It can be a stumbling block for many people. In my opinion, by presenting these principles as covenant guarantees and placing them in this order, Heavenly Father emphasizes that our human needs can indeed be met while keeping the law of chastity.

I'm sure you still have questions about keeping covenants, and that's completely fine. Please don't miss the last chapter on consecration. It is Heavenly Father's way of answering your questions and calming any remaining fears. For some, it is the law that's least recognizable, but it is also the most comforting.

Same-Sex Attraction and the Law of Chastity

The law of chastity does not need to be an obstacle to your relationship with God. It is, in fact, your lifeline to power, understanding, and a deeply personal connection to God. The promises God makes to you in the temple are no less effective than the promises He makes to anyone else. Covenants are how you will get what you want in a permanent way and overcome all that makes you afraid.

First, understand that your heavenly parents have great love and intelligence, so much so that they sent Christ to outmaneuver sin and death. Keeping your covenants brings that same love and intelligence to your aid in any situation you face.

With patience, and through Christ's step-by-step guidance, you are promised a fulfilling, joyful life. Sin negates this promise, but attraction does not. Your righteous journey will gently lead you to custom-fit opportunities, support, insights, and spiritual connectedness necessary to keep this promise, even while you feel attraction toward others.

Obeying the law of chastity does require abstinence from intimacy outside of marriage between a man and a woman. Before the many important questions start firing, remember that every covenant offers layers of reassurance to those who honor this commandment. Think about what fear is at the root of your question. Prayerfully consider whether one of the promises can alleviate the worry embedded in your question. Christ knows your questions and understands your fears. He gives us covenants to offer reliable answers (see Doctrine and Covenants 45:8–11).

The world outside the temple is saying you must choose between a happy life and a covenant relationship with God. The promises inside the temple boldly declare that you can have both. Don't underestimate Christ's ability to create your best outcome.

This reminds me of a story in the New Testament, found in Matthew 17:24–27. Tax collectors laid a trap for Jesus by accusing Him and Peter of not paying their taxes, thereby not showing allegiance to Ceaser (a symbol of worldly ideas). Christ escapes this trap in a way no one could have guessed, proving that God's solutions typically outmatch our mortal rationality.

He tells Peter to catch a fish, and in its mouth, he would find enough money for both their taxes. Peter does so, finds the money, and pays the tax. Christ proved that He did not have to choose between his identity as a lawful citizen of Judea and His identity as the Son of God. He could be both.

Jesus was teaching at least two lessons in this story.

Lesson 1: Jesus paid a tax that Peter had no way of paying himself. He demonstrated to the tax collectors that as the Christ, He was more powerful than the world. Worldly allegiances, currencies, assumptions, theories, or limitations did not apply to Him.

We all owe a tax for our citizenship in mortality. However, through His Atonement, Christ has paid this debt that we could not repay ourselves. We are all deeply indebted to our Savior for making mortality and exaltation possible. If we serve Him the way Peter did, we can all be reassured that our debts, worries, and fears will be resolved through Christ's immeasurable powers. There is no limitation in His ability to do this for us. Just as Peter could be a lawful Galilean and a follower of Christ, you can simultaneously be a lawful citizen of Zion and a mighty, joyful child of God.

Lesson 2: Why did Christ use a fish? He had lots of options. He could have crushed a rock with a gem inside or bloomed a flower filled with coins. Why a fish? I think it was because Peter identified as a fisherman. Fish were an essential part of Peter's life. It was a source of his temporal security, confidence, and purpose. For years, he had toiled night and day over fish. He was a fisherman, and in this moment, he was holding in one hand a fish and in the other, miraculous currency. Peter must have realized how much more power Jesus was offering him within his new identity as a disciple of Christ.

Your sexual attraction is an essential part of your life, ever-present night and day. Just as Christ did not pay taxes in the typical way, your path forward does not need to follow a typical route to be successful. Fear not your path. Doubt not your success (see Doctrine and Covenants 6:36). Just like Peter, Christ is offering you His partnership with a promise to lead you to personal fulfillment as a disciple of Christ. This partnership is so valuable that no other identifier can compare, in the same way that catching a fish cannot compare with blessing the lame to walk or restoring one who has died.

The law of chastity requires obedience to a standard of only married heterosexual relations. I do not pretend to understand how deeply this impacts your life. However, the Spirit prompts me to apply eternal truth with confidence and comprehensiveness. Any other effort would be disrespectful to you and ultimately unhelpful. Declare to Christ your covenantal intentions, give Him your offering, and prove Christ now herewith if He will not open a way for you to follow Him that is righteous, authentic, and joyful (see Malachi 3:10; 2 Peter 1:2–11).

When Christ taught truths that were difficult to apply, many of His followers chose to leave Him. He then inquired after His disciples, "Will ye also go away?"

Peter's reply to this question represents a hinge point within the New Testament: "Then Simon Peter answered him, 'Lord, to whom shall we go? thou hast the words of eternal life. And we believe and are sure that thou art that Christ, the Son of the living God'" (John 6:67–69).

After this declaration, the disciples began to fulfill their role as Apostles more boldly. Peter, James, and John were endowed with power on the Mount of Transfiguration and were given the ability to perform the same miracles Christ had performed.

Peter was indeed married, though he was often separated from his family in missionary travels. James was married but was martyred at a young age. John may have married later in life, but he outlived all his family. It is believed that many of the other Apostles never married, including Peter's brother, Andrew, and Jesus's brother, James. All these men sacrificed for Christ in different ways within their personal relationships. All led their own individual path. All were grateful for their dedication to Christ until their last days. Each of these Apostles changed the world by teaching us the value of Christ's partnership.

What is being asked of you is a dear and heavy sacrifice. Your choice to honor the law of chastity will offer a modern example of how every sacrifice for God is well worth the effort. I honor you in these efforts. In this way, you elevate the value of Christ's partnership in the minds of all who will learn of your faith. Your covenant-keeping will help teach our society to better understand the value of Christ's partnership. Then can great strides in spiritual progress be made, preparing us for the Second Coming of Jesus Christ.

While your path may be tailored to you individually, diverse Latter-day Saints can testify that Christ has led them to joy while they have still honored the law of chastity. We have and will continue to witness these authentic life stories more and more frequently. The Holy Ghost is inspiring added support systems and better perspectives, and unquestioningly declaring the love of God upon you.

Chastity and the Plan of Salvation

The endowment ordinance is a representation of the plan of salvation. When the plan of salvation is drawn in a primary class, it is typically shown on a linear path in some variation of the following:

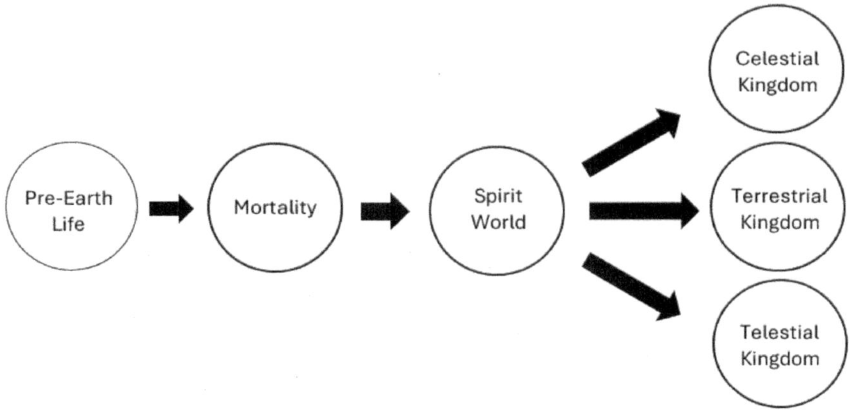

While this example is easier to understand for those newly learning this important concept, it is not complete. It disregards some of the most poignant parts within the plan of salvation. Here is a better example of the plan of salvation found on the Church website (churchofjesuschrist.org):

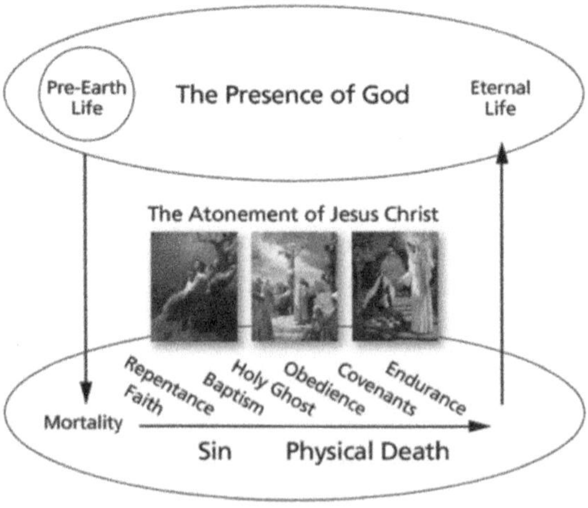

One key difference in the second illustration is how it highlights the vital role Jesus Christ plays within the plan. Even a quick visual makes it clear that the plan is not possible without Him. He achieves His objectives by offering physical laws—the Atonement, Resurrection, and exaltation—to make our plan of salvation work.

But there is another significant difference I wish to highlight. The second illustration shows the plan of salvation as circular rather than linear.

A linear understanding of the plan of salvation leaves so many questions unanswered. Why does chastity matter so much? Why does gender matter so much? If I am loyal, honest, and kind, why does it matter who I marry?

I have been asked these genuine questions in numerous ways. These are such important discussions. I encourage you to ask every genuine question that comes to mind in your prayers, with your family, and with your church leaders. God has good answers for you, and He wants you to hear them. Spiritual questions can also be better understood by considering how they fit within the plan of salvation. Of course, you would need to be visualizing it correctly.

Think about Heavenly Father fulfilling His path around the circle. He was once created as a man, with a body of flesh and bone. He partnered with an eternal companion who had attributes and abilities He did not have. Together, they learned to obey eternal laws and live by eternal principles. They were judged to be honorable in the work they had completed, and I assume they completed a great deal of work thereafter.

This success gave them eternal powers and exalted bodies. Eventually, their powers and abilities were reliable enough and strong enough to include others in their path of salvation. This is where the circular part comes in.

You and I began as intelligences, forms that existed before our heavenly parents spiritually begot us. We had agency, but with limited abilities and influence (see Doctrine and Covenants 93:30). Our Heavenly Father was able to come to us and offer us a spiritual body. He promised each of us the opportunity to be like Him. We believed in Him and trusted in His ability to help us progress, as He did. He accomplished all He said He would. Our heavenly parents then authored our salvation by giving us spiritual life. Creating our spiritual bodies was a work of partnership we do not yet understand between an exalted man and an exalted woman (see The Family: A Proclamation to the World).

As formed spirit children of God, our work here on earth continues with a physical body, formed only by a male and a female. All people will be restored to their resurrected bodies, regardless of mortal choices. Those who have honored eternal truths will be added upon by degrees. Those who focused on celestial living will be granted a celestial body—newly exalted with exalted powers.[12] This, too, will be made by our heavenly parents, male and female. In this way, we can all become "begotten sons and daughters of God" (Doctrine and Covenants 76:24).

We cannot be saved if we cannot be born spiritually and physically. We cannot save others if we cannot be exalted. Our salvation can only work with each phase of bodily progress. Our progress depends on the pairing of male and female, the fidelity that exists between us and our heavenly parents, and the respect with which They honor human life.

Chastity and gender matter because they are essential elements within salvation and exaltation. Salvation reconciles every struggle, and exaltation rewards every sacrifice following the laws of chastity may require. Eternal families are worth the effort so much that we cannot yet comprehend the joy that is possible.

The highest promise we are given is the promise that we can become like our heavenly parents. To be a god, you must have godly powers. To have godly powers, you must do godly work. To do godly work, you must "bring to pass the immortality and eternal life of man" (Moses 1:39). A god will look upon all the intelligences that remain with deep compassion (see Abraham 3:21–22). A god will gladly sacrifice himself to save them. This is the work and the glory of our God. These are the personal attributes our Heavenly Father is preparing within us by teaching us the laws of sacrifice, chastity, and consecration.

There are many aspects of exaltation we know little or nothing about yet. It is important not to make assumptions. We do know that man can become all that God currently is.[13] To be like Him, we will take on His purpose and divine ambition, completing the circle of salvation. We will grow and develop until we, too, are capable of fulfilling the divine promises our spirit children will depend on.

This is a time to practice the covenant powers of selflessness, commitment, and reliability. We do not need to be perfect, yet. There is still a great deal of learning to be done in this life and in the next. But we can at least understand why these covenant powers are important. There are a great many souls in need of our help. Our heavenly parents will help us, and we can learn how to better help Them.

Chapter 7

The Law of Consecration

Nephi III

Son of Nephi; grandson of Helaman
First ordained Apostle of the Americas
In the city of Bountiful
See 3 Nephi 8–12

Desperation is a dark emotion of being trapped with ineptitude and inability, surrounded by fearful circumstances, with no control over one's outcome. One feels the urge to claw, fight, and thrust it away, but man's arm is too weak to do so. In contrast, Christ has overcome desperation. He chose to accept mortality and succumb to His greatest fears, knowing it would allow Him to remove the sting from mine. Four times now, He has given Himself to save me.

Rescue from Fear

My mind returns to a fearful night thirty-four years ago. The unbelievers had gathered all those who had been faithful, me and my family among them, that they might take our lives the next morning (see 3 Nephi 1:1–12). The unbelievers—our neighbors—in their irrational shame, thought their unbelief could be blotted out by destroying those who believed in Christ.

The prophet—my father, Nephi II—was gone. I was still grieving him and struggling to understand how to fill my role as the leader of these Christian Saints in crisis.

Early that morning, I knelt in the darkness and lifted my head toward the sky. With all the energy of my soul, I pleaded with God for our safety all day long. Desperately fearing the setting of the sun, it was Christ's voice that comforted me: "Lift up your head and be of good cheer; for behold, the time is at hand, and on this night shall the sign be given, and on the morrow come I into the world, to show unto the world that I will fulfil all that which I have caused to be spoken by the mouth of my holy prophets" (3 Nephi 1:13).

Christ's daylight never dimmed. That glorious night, basking in His brightness, I learned who I could rely on for light. The sunshine of hope in my heart did not relent. I was saved from the desperation of fear because Christ fulfilled His commitment to be born in a great act of selfless condescension.

Rescue from Grief

For thirty-three years thereafter, I was strengthened in influence and leadership as a prophet to my people. My service was dedicated to the Lord. Angels ministered to me daily, strengthening my endurance and helping me stay focused on my responsibilities. My brother Timothy was my ever-stalwart companion in times of hardship and blessing. All I did was with his support and counsel.

At one point in our ministry, my brother and I were teaching a group of people when the city elders accused us of trespassing on their lands (see 3 Nephi 7:14–20). They dragged us to the foot of their temple, where they interrogated and mocked us. Bands of thugs beat us, then prepared for our stoning.

I was the first to be tied down to the ground. The crowd was too eager and began throwing stones before our captors could tie Timothy beside me. In the confusion, Timothy broke free and ran forward to shield me. Tied down, there was nothing I could do. Our captures didn't mind the spectacle.

As I watched my loyal brother give his final breath, my grief was agonizing. How could this have happened to us? Where were the angels we saw every day? Instead, Jesus did something I certainly did not expect. He saved me from my desperation in grief by sharing His power with me. *I* would save my brother.

While flat on the ground, wet with sweat and blood, I heard distinctly the words "Raise thy brother." My mind was a spinning cycle of anger, panic, and pain. I breathed in and out, struggling to grasp what was just said. Men came forward to confirm Timothy's death, then dragged him away by his arms.

"Raise thy brother." Even raising *myself* off the ground would be a miraculous feat.

But I had to believe I could. First, I raised one arm, then the other. The straps gave way as if I was never tied down. I crouched, then stood tall before the crowd.

I felt their thoughts. I felt their hatred. I sensed their version of desperation. They needed me to be wrong. If I weren't, then they must change and give up all their ill-gotten riches and pleasures. They would rather kill me than admit their false reality. At all costs, I must be wrong, and Christ must be a myth.

I would hear no more of their mockery. With a voice of authority, in the name of Jesus Christ, I called my brother's name. I commanded that he arise and come forth. As Timothy moved upon the ground, the crowd let out a cry of astonishment and fear.

My brother rose to his feet, fully alive and fully healed. His first words, spoken in a powerful voice, declared that Jesus was the Christ, the Savior who would soon come with love and power. I learned my life held greater purpose than I knew before.

Rescue from Sin

One year ago, early in the morning, I was returning home, passing through a mountainous village I knew well. These people were not violent in their dissent; they were just indifferent to my continual pleadings.

Without even a momentary warning, the ground shook with a momentary ripple effect across the earth. I balanced myself and continued to walk till I felt the rumble again. Not unfamiliar with earth-shakings, I stooped down to wait.

Then came a terrible sound like the crushing of boulders cascading down a hillside. The horizon above the hills suddenly grew with a cast of rusty haze, then ashen gray. Dark, heavy clouds rumbled from the north with unexpected force, corrupting the morning sky. I sensed catastrophe lurching toward me, just over the hills that blocked my view. As a strong, hot wind picked up, I felt a deep urgency to be back with my family.

The sky changed dramatically and quickly over the next several minutes. The last morning rays hid away in the clouds, and lightning cracked across the sky like an executioner's signature. Tree limbs bent, and dust from the fields streaked the air. The Great Storm of God had begun.

I ran toward town headlong into ash-black rain. I yelled to everyone I saw: "Get away from here! Run for higher ground!" I pleaded, "Save your family."

The ground continued to rumble, so people reluctantly began streaming out of town and up the surrounding hills. Those who refused slammed their doors and arrogantly lit their fires. I scrambled up the steep hillside with a thin trail of people following behind, hail now pelting our backs.

Up ahead, overgrown and neglected, was a small church. It once served as an outpost of prayer. Children had long ago stolen its stones from its walls. It was, after all, the younger generation who fell away so soon after the signs of the Savior's birth. Perhaps some of those same children, grown with young families, were now crouching with me in the rain.

The earth began shaking violently as if she wished to fling us off. Unable to stand, we had nowhere else to go. The air was choked with a haze that shimmered in my eyes, dimming the light. With great intensity, the ground heaved, and I saw what I thought were everlasting hills crumble like sand.

Someone cried out, and I turned to see that a fire had started in town. Despite all the rain, the fire spread swiftly and with purpose. As I sat and watched, I could not hear them, but I imagined the screams of panic as families escaped from their thatched-roofed homes.

This was not a typical fire. White flames tinged with royal blue were both beautiful and terrible. Was I watching the finger of God reach out of the sky to ignite the fires Himself?

Over the next long hour, I began to accept that this was the storm marking the death of the Messiah. Reading prophecies was so tame compared to experiencing them. Through miracles and prophecy, through signs and wonders, through every seed of faith within me, I had tried to teach people of Christ. I could have moved a mountain more easily than their minds. God was now moving the mountains Himself.

Still, the storm raged, with lightning and thunder striking frequently. The rocks collided, and the creek flooded. As I thought it could not possibly continue, it simply did. Hillsides collapsing to the north, fissures opening to the south, carefully cultivated farms were ruined. Every flame represented someone's pride; every rumble would cause another person to fall.

Finally, oh finally! The rumbling of earth and sky began to quiet. It was as if the storm had stuttered. The brief reprieve was wasted as people screamed their anger up toward God. Why did this happen? They wanted to know. What were they supposed to do now?

I could understand how they felt: so exposed, so surprised. Even I did not expect the destruction laid to waste before us.

"Do you want our wretchedness?" It wasn't a yell but a whisper. And it was mine.

Despite all the miracles I had performed and all the angels I had seen, this overwhelming experience uncovered a deep, unresolved pocket of distrust within my soul. Does God still love us even now?

I felt like I was learning from the beginning all over again. Momentarily, I forgot the wisdom of my Maker. In my desperation, I forgot that everything God does furthers our redemption. I reacted with pride as if God owed me something.

The earth awoke again like a giant whose heavy hand arose to smack the far side of our hill. I was nothing but a pebble on its surface. The dirt heaved upward, then over the giant fingers like water. I, along with everyone else, careened downward, tangled in an avalanche of tree limbs and rockslides. I had thought the fire wouldn't stop till everything was consumed. I was wrong. The giant buried the fire, along with my only source of light. We were left scattered down the slope.

Though it must have been mid-morning, a dark veiling mist billowed forth from the canyon. How quickly it went to pitch! It felt like the sun had died and the earth was rejecting us.

I heard people calling out, and I was grateful so many had survived. Their grief was rising in the dark. It was difficult to process a complete lack of control or stability. Our ability to improve our situation was extremely limited.

At some point, the earth still shuddered but finally quieted back to sleep. I tried to help, comfort, and heal those I found, but every source of food or water was buried. Every passing hour of thirst, hunger, and grief just blended.

I kept asking why. I kept trying to determine what Christ's purpose was. This storm marked the death of our Savior. Despair hit as I realized that His voice was not coming to comfort me that night. Jesus Christ was lying dead in a foreign, faraway land.

On perhaps the second night of pitch-black, I was trying to comfort an older woman. She was dying, and there was nothing I could do. I told her how sorry I was. She touched my face to ensure I was looking toward her and said, "Right now, we are in a world without Christ. Do not be sorry for me. I'm going to where I can find Him again."

She was right! This storm also marked the fact that His sacrifice was complete. He had not exempted Himself from this suffering. He had let Himself die, too. This trapped feeling with no options is what Christ was trying (has always been trying!) to save us from. This is what life would be like without Him! How could we fully understand the goodness of His presence without feeling the desperation of our separation?

Desperation welled inside like never before. I understood the words of my namesake: "O wretched man that I am!" (2 Nephi 4:16–24) While short-sighted, I had voiced my doubts, I had trembled in fear, and forgotten to Whom I belong. Why did I have to be pushed to the point of desperation before understanding how comprehensively Jesus Christ can save us?

Christ rescued me by uncovering every pocket of doubt within me till I no longer reacted in sin. I repented of my doubts, redoubled my gratitude for His salvation, and fully released my pride.

By the third day, I was longing for the face I had seen in visions and the voice I had heard before. When I finally heard Him, a cry of utter relief and gratitude escaped from me. The weight of being without Him was lifted from my shoulders, and I dropped to the ground, having expended all my strength in just three days of being alone.

His voice had the power to pierce my ears and grip my heart. He spoke of falling, again and again, fallen … fallen … fallen. He spoke of desolation, like a great fissure that could swallow us whole without His firm foundation. After the storm, I better understood what He meant. But He also spoke of His relentless attempts to gather, nourish, and spare (see 3 Nephi 10:4–7). Surviving that long night strengthened my motivation to be under His soft wing forevermore.

Rescue from Failure

The sun rose the next morning, and I was able to return home to search out my family. God had spared His faithful and humble followers. The work of succoring the afflicted, rebuilding our homes, securing our needs, and healing our minds and bodies took a great deal of time. Yet we were comforted by Christ's message spoken in the dark.

He had repeatedly confirmed our lineage within the house of Israel and confirmed that God's covenants to our fathers were still in place. We better understood that these ancient covenants held protective power over us across all distance and time. We kept our hearts open to the further direction that He promised would come.

My family and many others felt eager to gather as one. I spread word of my intentions to travel to the temple at Bountiful, inviting all to join with me. Christ's voice had come to us, and now we wanted to go to Christ. The Spirit drew us to the temple.

What a magnificent reward to hear yet another voice from heaven! In the dark, we had heard the voice of Christ, but at the temple we heard a voice even more grand, more reverent, and more powerful. One I had not heard before. It came softly, gently, and repetitively, not wanting to overpower but still signifying the importance of what was to be said. We heard these glorious words: "Behold my Beloved Son, in whom I am well pleased, in whom I have glorified my name—hear ye Him" (3 Nephi 11:7).

The Mighty God, Elohim to the Ancient of Days, even my own spiritual Father, spoke to me with His own voice. Even after all we had witnessed, the power of the Godhead manifest unto us in our flesh was more than we could stand. Overcome with humility for the power and love within that voice, my body and spirit reacted in immediate worship for the One who spoke.

Raising my head and turning upward, I saw the Son descending from above. This is the Man who had saved me, taught me, and comforted me for so many years. I knew His face.

In His glory, He had placed the wicked where they could learn better and succored the weak so they could witness Him. In His glory, He pronounced His work accomplished and declared Himself the Son of God. Finally, I heard what I wanted so badly but dared not imagine. In His glory, my Lord called my name.

I rose slowly but surely, climbing the steps of the temple to stand before Him. He looked upon me, eye to eye, heart to heart. I had thought my eyes would draw away from His out of humility or even shame. But I did not feel the urge to do so because of my complete trust in His ability to redeem me. I was indeed imperfect, but because I was with Him, I had never been safer. Instead, my eyes were full of love for this glorious Man.

His gaze held the emotion of all I had experienced. He was indeed sad about my struggles, but I also felt the validation of every promise He had ever made to me. Every truth He had inspired was confirmed in my heart. I had taught those truths as boldly as I could. To feel that I had aided Him in some way—to feel His gratitude—made my heart ring with fulfillment.

Next, He called my brother, Timothy, to stand beside me. In what thrilled my soul, He called my eldest son, Jonas, to stand with us and nine others whom I consider my brothers in Christ. He placed His hands on each of us and bestowed on us His authority to serve and teach the people on His behalf. He offered us His kingdom, even His power.

And that was when I recognized rescue number four: with His partnership, I cannot fail.

At His call, heavenly angels came and ministered to my people. I watched them gather the children. Watching my young son Nephi held within those angelic arms, I became undone. I wept as a child, shaking with gratitude, with tears of joy streaming down my face.

Christ stood before me in the flesh. I felt the wound on His side, the scars of love in the palms of His hands and in His wrists. I worshipped Him. "My heart was broken, and you healed me. My spirit was desperate, and you saved me. My soul belongs to thee."

With sincerity and gentleness, He asked me, "Do you give it freely?" In joyful reverence, I bowed my head. "Yes."

Receiving Fulfillment

Just as Nephi endured, we have been warned of increasingly intense hardship as the Second Coming draws closer. Yet, we can be reassured that through our temple covenants, we can still receive what we desire, just as Nephi did. The law of consecration is your commitment to offer nothing less than everything you have to the Lord. The promise received is that He will provide you with nothing less than everything He has.

There is a powerful lesson to be learned from the life of Nephi III. He lived through intense hardship, not only from the hands of others but also through the wrath of Christ during the great storm. Yet even then, his fears were all addressed, and his righteous desires were all granted. This chart offers a few examples of Nephi's fears and how Christ answered them.

Fear	**Answer**
God, do you hear me? Are you real?	Receives revelation and hears Christ's voice
Can I trust you?	Is given promises of fulfillment by Christ
Do they hate us? Will they kill us?	Christ's birth and a full night of sunlight
Will I be alone? Am I good enough?	Raises Timothy from death (a symbol of Christ)
Will my family be safe?	Ministering angels bless all the children
Will my family be happy?	Jonas is given power as an Apostle
How will I know what to do?	Receives the gift of the Holy Ghost
Will I be happy?	Is granted his greatest wish

The record states explicitly that Nephi received what he wanted most. Just after being called as an Apostle in Christ's Church, Nephi and the other Apostles were asked to teach the people His word. They were then invited to be baptized, Nephi being the first: "And they did pray for that which they most desired; and they desired that the Holy Ghost should be given unto them. … And it came to pass when they were all baptized and had come up out of the water, the Holy Ghost did fall upon them, and they were filled with the Holy Ghost and with fire. And behold, they were encircled about as if it were by fire; and it came down from heaven, and the multitude did witness it, and did bear record; and angels did come down out of heaven and did minister unto them" (3 Nephi 19:9–14).

Recognize the order here. Nephi sincerely wanted something. He prayed to God for direction. He committed to God in a covenant partnership. Then he served the people, and finally received what he wanted most: The gift of the Holy Ghost. But Christ gifted them even more than they could have expected with the ministering of angels: "While the angels were ministering unto the disciples, behold, Jesus came and stood in the midst and ministered unto them" (3 Nephi 19:15). These early Saints were blessed directly by Christ.

This pattern is a tight summary of the eternal law of consecration. As you serve in righteousness, you will receive abundantly. Hardships as severe as earthquakes, utter darkness, volcanoes, storms, and even violence are not strong enough to take these blessings away from you.

Why does Christ do what He does? What does Christ want? What makes Him joyful? He lived the law of consecration.

He answered this question while teaching Nephi and the other newly called Apostles of the Americas: "Therefore, what manner of men ought ye to be? Verily I say unto you, even as I am. … And verily I say unto you, whatsoever things ye shall ask the Father in my name shall be given unto you. Therefore, ask, and ye shall receive; knock, and it shall be opened unto you; for he that asketh, receiveth; and unto him that knocketh, it shall be opened. And now, behold, my joy is great, even unto fulness, because of you, and also this generation; yea, and even the Father rejoiceth, and also all the holy angels, because of you and this generation; for none of them are lost; … and in them I have fulness of joy" (3 Nephi 27:27–31).

For all His effort and all His sacrifice, He wants to share His power to help you become even as He is. Only after such a transformation can Christ always have His forever family *with Him*. Would you not do all in your power to receive such a blessing?

As you consecrate your life to doing those things that bring Christ joy (such as loving God and loving His children), then He will empower you to find a fulness of joy also. If you help build up God's kingdom, then you will become a joint heir of God's kingdom. You will gain access to godly success: long-lasting, fulfilling, customized, empowering, even miraculous success.

The last lesson Christ taught before ascending into heaven was to ask His newly called Nephite Apostles, "What is it that ye desire of me?" (3 Nephi 28:1; see also 2 Chronicles 1:1–12; Psalm 27:4; Doctrine and Covenants 7:1–8). In the Old Testament, Christ asked this same question to Solomon after he sacrificed at the ancient tabernacle of the congregation. In the New Testament, Christ asked this question to His Apostles in Jerusalem and confirmed it through revelation to Joseph Smith in the Doctrine and Covenants. In every book of scripture, Christ teaches us to look forward with hope to receiving our deepest desires—if we also develop a charitable heart and a covenant relationship with God. The law of consecration is assurance that Christ's generous blessings can apply to you as well.

Sharing in Christ's Powers

Nearly every missionary I know strives to live the law of consecration as best they can. Their service to others and dedication to Christ's pure gospel never fail to inspire me. It is their selfless priorities that create a special spirit about them. A favorite passage has been memorized by missionaries for decades, helping develop their dedication to the work. It is the short and powerful section of Doctrine and Covenants 6.

These verses certainly offer excellent motivation for missionary work, but that's not all—it's a summary of the law of consecration: charity, effort, reward. As a keystone covenant, it upholds all five covenants for the saving of your own soul and the souls of others.

2 Therefore, **O ye that embark in the service of God, see that ye serve Him with all your heart, might, mind and strength[5]**, that ye may stand blameless before God at the last day.

Temple reference

4 For behold the field is white already to harvest; and lo, **he that thrusteth in his sickle with his might[5]**, the same layeth up in store that he perisheth not, but **bringeth salvation to his soul;**

5 And **faith[1], hope[2], charity[5] and love[3], with an eye single to the glory of God[4]**, qualify him for the work.

[1] Law of Obedience
[2] Law of Sacrifice
[3] Law of the Gospel
[4] Law of Chastity
[5] Law of Consecration

Powers of Christ gained through covenant

6 Remember **faith, virtue, knowledge, temperance, patience, brotherly kindness, godliness, charity, humility, diligence**.

7 **Ask, and ye shall receive; knock, and it shall be opened unto you.** Amen.

Temple endowment

As you go to the temple seeking sacred connection with God, you symbolically knock, and the veil will open to you. You will be taught that by worthily invoking the priesthood authority of God's five covenants, you can be welcomed into His presence. In this way, God is symbolically confirming to you that your deepest desires are within your reach.

The law of consecration promises that as you give everything you have to Christ, He will share everything He has with you. It is the most incredible deal you will ever be offered. But still, it doesn't end there. As Brother Bradley R. Wilcox, former first counselor in the Young Men General Presidency, shared, "It would be easy for Heavenly Father to simply give you all that He has. He desires to help you become all that He is. Thus, your commitments demand more of you because that is how God is making more of you."[14]

Gaining what you want most is not the end of the covenant power-sharing process. It is not done until the effort of service, testimony, charity, and the gathering of Israel has created the necessary pressure to stimulate change within you. It is not done until Christ's eternal

Atonement has fully refined your character. Then you can truly become as God is.

HOW TO SHARE CHRIST'S POWER WITH OTHERS

Christ wants all His brothers and sisters to be safe, knowledgeable, and loved. This is the focus of the gathering of Israel. Your success depends on how much you support others in achieving theirs. Therefore, it falls on us, those baptized into the noble birthright, to turn our hearts in love toward our brothers and sisters (see Doctrine and Covenants 2).

Charity is the pure love of Christ, yet charity requires sacrifice and empathy. It takes consecrated work and a lifetime of refining practice to learn how to love fully and consistently. Loving as God loves is a crucial step to becoming like God.

In the law of consecration, you promise to dedicate all your "might, mind, and strength" toward building the kingdom of God (see Doctrine and Covenants 59; see also Moroni 10:30–33; Mosiah 2:11, 17–22). But what is the effect of this work? More unity, refuge, and peace. Covenants don't protect us from betrayal or heartache, but they counter the vulnerability these experiences can cause. Our personal charity creates an environment where others can also experience the love of God. They can feel less vulnerable while with us and therefore less susceptible to Satan's manipulations. As you build up the kingdom of God, gather the house of Israel, and support the ordained prophet, Christ's power-sharing spreads from person to person. Perhaps this is why our prophet has put so much emphasis on engaging in this work, stating, "The Lord is hastening His work to gather Israel. That gathering is the most important thing taking place on earth today. Nothing else compares in magnitude, nothing else compares in importance, nothing else compares in majesty."[15]

Consider how covenants cause ripple effects that reverberate on both sides of the veil. Imagine what happens as every covenant-keeping soul combines efforts to share the good news of Christ. Fear dissipates, confidence grows, charity multiplies, and resilience flourishes. Covenants bring healing and peace, whether in mortality or the spirit world.

Every covenant made and kept diminishes the influence of Satan and increases the impact of Jesus Christ. The result is fewer temptations to distract, fewer traumas to overcome, more believers who can teach, more ministering angels who can serve, more perspectives to learn from, and more unity to enjoy. This power-sharing process will someday scale worldwide. A consecrated effort to support the making and keeping of covenants is the only way eternal families and world peace can be achieved (see 1 John 5:1–5; Alma 37:43–47). Indeed, it is the only work with the authority and longevity to do so. I testify that covenants will be the means whereby the atrocities of the past are healed, and the tyrannies of the future are avoided.

Love God and Love His Children

Christ has taught the ideals of the law of consecration so many times that it would be difficult for me to include them all. In His most well-known sermons, Christ has promised all we could want in return for righteousness and charity. In every instance, it's made perfectly clear that gaining what we want cannot and will not be separated from our desire to serve others. Godly powers will only accompany a godly love of God's children.

The Sermon on the Mount is an example of the law of consecration being taught in detail. A careful study of 3 Nephi 12–14 is especially worthwhile. Christ emphasized the Sermon on the Mount twice: first, to the Apostles in Galilee—the same men who would willingly die in their effort to spread faith—and second, to the Saints gathered in the Americas—the same people who would embrace consecration and live in blessed peace for centuries.

There is one difference between the sermon recorded in the Bible and the sermon recorded in the Book of Mormon: the phrase "come unto me." This significant phrase is fulfilled at the veil in the temple of God. I interpret this phrase to mean that the blessings specified in the Sermon on the Mount are found through a covenant relationship with Jesus Christ. He is teaching us that He knows what we want, He knows how we can get it, and He has the power to give it, but we must come unto Him to receive what He offers.

Blessed Are	For They Shall	Outcome
The poor in spirit	Obtain the kingdom of heaven	Power
They that weep now	Laugh	Joy
They that mourn	Be comforted	Peace
The meek	Inherit the earth	Abundance
They which do hunger and thirst	Be filled	Fulfillment
The merciful	Obtain mercy	Protection
The pure in heart	See God	Knowledge
The peacemakers	Be called the children of God	Family
They which are persecuted	Obtain the kingdom of heaven	Power

He is teaching us that God will provide for our needs (see Matthew 6:31–33, Luke 6:19–36), that we can inherit from our Heavenly Father (see Joseph Smith Translation, Matthew 7:17 [in the Bible appendix]), and that we can trust Him to keep His promises (see Matthew 7:24–25). Christ repeated this sermon, knowing how powerful the law of consecration can be in building our hope and overcoming our fears. It includes all that is grand and powerful.

After only three days of learning from Christ, the warring Lamanites and Nephites disregarded over 600 years of conflict. They built a perfect peace that lasted for 200 years. Such a transformation can't happen unless these people trusted Christ to overcome their every vulnerability, calm their every fear, and keep His every promise.

They finally realized they did not need to compete with their brothers and sisters. They understood they had an abundance of love and resources. Christ was the source of all they truly wanted, and He shared abundantly. Generosity could then feel easy, and selfishness could feel unreasonable. They relied on Christ and the Holy Ghost, realizing that every other source of security was a crutch. Their peace was long-lasting because they were finally unified in a successful strategy.

"And it came to pass that there was no contention in the land, because of the love of God which did dwell in the hearts of the people.

And there were no envyings, nor strifes, nor tumults, nor whoredoms, nor lyings, nor murders, nor any manner of lasciviousness; and surely there could not be a happier people among all the people who had been created by the hand of God. There were no robbers, nor murderers, neither were there Lamanites, nor any manner of -ites; but they were in one, the children of Christ, and heirs to the kingdom of God" (4 Nephi 1:15–17).

The law of consecration worked for these people because they saw with their own eyes how comprehensively Christ loved a large and diverse group of people. They saw firsthand how His love healed those they loved and even transformed those they once hated. They witnessed Him cure such a large variety of ailments, frustrations, fears, habits, and doubts. They trusted Him more than they ever had before. Spiritual hesitation was dispelled; they committed themselves fully to Christ. Each of these people felt the sublime love of Jesus Christ in its potency. A love so powerful that modern witnesses of Jesus Christ have never been able to find the words to describe it adequately.

For the Nephites and Lamanites, their understanding of who Christ is and what He can do was greatly expanded to the extent that they were no longer afraid to give their full commitment. They stopped trying to get what they wanted from unworthy, ineffective sources. They had no more motivation to do evil (see Mosiah 5:1–5). Their only motivation was to be "heirs to the kingdom of God."

In what ways do you compete with others? Do you rely more on your own defenses or the promises of Jesus Christ? Is your sense of security based on your circumstances or your covenants? The answers to these questions impact your ability to be united, charitable, and resilient. As you consider how you could be better consecrated to God, think of how He can be your source of security, regardless of your to-do list, budget, health, social status, or circumstances. Relying on Christ will make your consecrated service more generous and more genuine.

Christ's Dying Wish

Just before Christ entered the Garden of Gethsemane, He closed His mortal ministry by dedicating it to God in the great Intercessory Prayer. He knew He was about to fight the greatest battle of human history and to offer Himself as the greatest sacrifice of love. At this sacred time, He gathered His faithful disciples around Him and said the following to His Father:

"And now come I to thee; and these things I speak in the world, that they might have my joy fulfilled in themselves. … Neither pray I for these alone, but for them also which shall believe on me through their word; that they all may be one; as thou, Father, art in me, and I in thee, that they also may be one in us: that the world may believe that thou hast sent me" (John 17: 13, 20–21).

His wish is that we may be joyfully fulfilled through Him, but unity seems to be a critical component. His desire for our unity is expressed repeatedly, in multiple ways throughout this sacred benediction. He is praying not just for the ancient Saints but also for us Latter-day Saints: "them also which shall believe." His great plea on our behalf is that we will all be united as "one." In this way, Christ's joy may be felt by us all, and all may share Christ's gifts.

As the Good Shepard contemplated what would be the next needed step for His flock, He thought of unity. Unity was the bridge He imagined between the covenant principles He taught and what we could then become. His followers in the Americas fulfilled Christ's dying wish. They unified themselves, and we have a record of the outcome—blessed peace. Unity will help the promises of God feel real to those who are struggling in our day. Unity will make it easier to imagine ourselves as children of God in a divine family.

Every covenant brings us a step closer to unity. For example:

- Step 1: Christ's power is better seen when the obedient describe how Christ's commandments make them feel safe.
- Step 2: Christ's power is better gained when those who sacrifice express gratitude for the opportunity to serve.
- Step 3: Christ's power is better retained when the repentant testify of the goodness of God, His mercy, and His wisdom.
- Step 4: Christ's power is better increased when the chaste honor God with their loyalty.
- Step 5: Christ's power is better shared when the humble servant gives of themself in consecrated love of God and His children.

In this way, unity becomes the great multiplier of Christ's power. In this way, preparation to meet God can extend to everyone.

I ask you, in honor of my Savior whom I love, to take the steps necessary to receive the security of your endowment. I ask you, in honor of the hope He has taught me, to attend the temple more often and with intention. I ask you, in honor of my children and your children, to study these covenant principles within the scriptures. Rely on them. Live them. Teach them. They will increase the joy within your life. They will uplift the trajectory of your family. Your efforts to worship within the temple will have a positive effect on us all.

Conclusion

The Restoration

Peter

Formerly known as Simon
First Apostle of Jesus Christ
Along the bank of the Susquehanna River, Pennsylvania
See Joseph Smith History 1;
Doctrine and Covenants 107; 110; 128

When I was a fisherman, I would sit beside the Sea of Galilee to ponder and strategize as best I could. I was living on the edge of survival in many ways. I had limited knowledge and, therefore, limited choices. Life was fleeting—in harsh conditions, among people of poor means, under the rule of Roman oppressors. Who was I to change my conditions? Who was I to make a mark on history? I could barely provide for my family and pay my taxes.

Following John the Baptist along the River Jordan gave me hope. His words filled me with wonder that God would indeed offer a Messiah and that He would live in our time. My belief in God was a way to calm my mind and cope with all the factors I couldn't control. Without the coming of Jesus Christ, that is all my belief would ever be. But I wanted control. I wanted the power to break free from my shackles and fill my cup to the brim. But such things were not possible. Sitting at the edge of the sea, I was just one Jewish man among so many, scratching at the promises I had been taught as a child.

I was desperate enough to fish every night in black waters, even though I couldn't swim. I was consumed with figuring out how to bring food home every day, every week, and every month. I stressed over the need to protect my small family from injustice and unpredictability. That was the extent of my hopes. I had no further vision of who or what I could be. I knew I was nothing but small, and it made me react in small ways.

But when Jesus Christ walked into my view, my vision began to stretch. He was a man not easily forgotten, even by those who did not know who He was. Tall, assured, and focused, He commanded your eyes to follow Him as He walked by. The men of my day were never so noble and never had so much to accomplish. They could not even imitate such a demeanor.

Jesus never flinched in fear or overreacted in stress. He never faltered in his priorities or lost sight of the greater purpose. He only sought God and acted in accordance with the holy word He received. He knew He was the Son of God. He never let those with limited vision change His understanding of who He was.

I was one of limited vision, discipline, education, and prudence, yet He still chose me as His Apostle. Lesson by lesson, my Messiah removed the limitations of my vision. He taught me those truths on which worlds do rest. He taught me the humility of knowing God's will without doubt. I could see His interactions change the people around me. I learned to acknowledge God's handiwork through me. Finally, I allowed His Spirit to enter my heart and release all my hesitancy.

But still, I have regrets. Yes, I slept in the Garden of Gethsemane, seeking the dream where the sublime Savior of my existence was not about to die. Yes, I drew my sword, once again reacting out of fear, knowing Christ could protect Himself, but instinctively knowing that *I* could not survive without Him. Yes, I denied my Redeemer three times. Had I been imprisoned, I could not be a proper witness to His Resurrection, for I would not have witnessed His death.

Christ was doing His work, and He made it abundantly clear that I was to let Him do His work. Even given His close attention, I could not yet grasp the glory of each drop of blood or each groan of pain. Even faced with His glorious sacrifice, I was selfishly thinking of my own devastation—the pain I would feel during every minute without Him, the gaping pit that would be left in my soul, the glorious vision of the future suddenly gone dark.

Nothing but shadows existed for three days. Nothing but memories, tearful eyes, and unanswered questions. Why did I not accept the comfort within His preparations? Why did I not realize then the purpose He had described for me? Because to do so, I would have had to accept my responsibilities in His plans. This was nearly impossible for a lowly fisherman who, only three years earlier, was incapable of envisioning real healings, multiple resurrections, glorified transfiguration, and my own foreordination. To lead without Him, to be an example of His way, to use the keys of His power—it was more than I had the capacity to bear. I focused on my grief, and it took time to grapple with my duty.

My Savior enlarged my capability as He promised He would. He empowered me through my learned humility and supplication. He led me with clarity and focus, just as He had been led with clarity and focus. Learning to increase my capacity was an internal struggle that required me to accept who I truly am: not a son of man but a son of God, a prophet of the Messiah.

Jesus Christ has completed the wondrous task of uniting me with my true self. I am not, nor have I ever been, just a lowly fisherman. This has always been such a small part of my identity. I am a man of greater stature and knowledge than I could have possibly imagined when pondering upon the seashore in Galilee. Jesus Christ, my friend, reintroduced me to myself. I am the messenger who taught our first parents, Adam and Eve, the covenants of salvation. Jesus Christ, my Savior, restored to my remembrance that I am a man who can command Satan to depart. Jesus Christ, my Redeemer, showed me that I am a man who can worship in the presence of Elohim. Jesus Christ, my King, has now authorized me to usher in the restoration of His higher power upon the earth in these latter days.

As I sit pondering along this Susquehanna River, the same way I used to on the banks of Galilee centuries ago, there are two men nearby who do not yet fully understand their true identities. Among other things, I have been tasked with expanding their vision a little further.

They are praying, seeking spiritual preparation and divine revelation from God. I know the feeling well. I understand their eagerness, mixed with apprehension, over how this new enlightenment might disrupt their current understanding. Yet God will not call His work complete until all His children come to fully understand who they truly are, free from misperceptions and limitations.

Joseph Smith and Oliver Cowdery must embrace who they truly are so that others in this generation can also come to understand who *they* can truly become. I will bestow upon them the holy power of the Son of God, for Christ wants His power to spread and wants His message shared. Joseph and Oliver cannot yet see how many brothers and sisters will hear of their expanded vision and believe their words.

Joseph understands he has been chosen, as I once was, but he does not yet understand the trust Jesus has in him. I, too, understand the weight of expectation when Jesus Christ asks His work to be done. At first, I also felt the sting of self-doubt and incapability, at times so strong it paralyzed me. I was only able to make progress once I began to rely on the keys of the priesthood bestowed upon me. Joseph will learn to use these keys wisely and honorably, just as I have. Joseph and I will continue in the work of Jesus Christ, for we are His prophets. It was my role to offer Christ's gospel to the Jews and the Gentiles. It is now Joseph's role to offer Christ's restored gospel to the entire world.

All honor belongs to the author of honor, God the Father. Joseph will need boldness to fulfill all that God has for him. Many will not understand God's urgency. Many will not understand the drastic change that will be necessary. Their vision is not as broad. Their ears will be distracted from God's promises by mortal limitations.

Regardless, Joseph must move forward as Christ directs. He must attempt what feels impossible because the impossible is what God requires. Each time Joseph follows through on Christ's commands, the people will see more clearly into Christ's intentions, as my people did. When the priesthood was lost in my day, the people's vision once again began to narrow, but I am here to restore priesthood power for the last time—never to be removed, never to be lost. There will forevermore be people worthy to hold and expand the work of Jesus Christ with full hearts and clear vision.

Joseph must not doubt that he can do far more influential things than just walking on water. Through the priesthood power he will soon hold, and through the future restoration of God's covenants, he will have the power to impact one's eternity while still in mortality. He will hold the power to unite people with their true selves. I declare unto you that Joseph Smith will be the first elder of this dispensation, disbursing from his hands the authorization to enact Christ's work.

Again and forever, I testify of the divinity of Jesus Christ. I have witnessed His marvelous glory from the first dispensation to the last. I know of His power to transform, for I have been transformed. I see His vision of the future. It cannot be realized without the enacting of priesthood power unto the establishment of covenantal promises between God and man. I am here to spread the covenants taught to Adam and Eve. I am here to connect them with the covenants made with my forefathers, Abraham, Issac, and Jacob. I am here to honor the promises I made to my own people. I am here to ensure that these sacred covenants can be offered to every member of the house of Israel and every Gentile until each has their opportunity to declare Jesus as the Christ, the Son of the living God.

I have come to further the Messiah's work of transforming us all.

My Time in the Temple

Transformation comes slowly to a stubborn heart such as mine. It has taken me a very long time to pause before I react. It has taken me a very long time to recognize that there are better ways to handle a situation than my first reaction. Three years ago, I knew there were ideas about the temple that I had to get down on paper, yet I felt I was inadequate to do so. To calm my anxiety, I sought as much time in the temple as I could manage as an ordinance worker and a patron.

Nearly every week in the temple, fellow temple workers told me about a faith-building experience they had. The building of their faith has built mine. The ripple effects spread far and wide.

May I take this opportunity to share with you just a few experiences of my own that have touched me recently? They mark some points of transformation in my heart; points where I have let go of something I did not need and held more tightly to Christ, whom I need dearly.

I understand that many feel their sacred experiences are not to be shared. I respect that and also act in that way. I hold close those experiences that would be difficult for me to explain to someone else accurately. For example, those experiences that hinge on a deep understanding of my internal thoughts would not serve someone else well. But I feel strongly that when God touches my life, it is meant to benefit others, as well as myself.

When my father was a young boy, he and his younger brother were saved from drowning by a prompting that came to my grandfather half a mile away. In many ways, it was as if I were pulled from the water that day. When I shared the story of quitting my job in New York, that miracle was not meant to impact just my first daughter, but also my second and my third, and their second and their third.

Miracles are a gift to the many, not just one. When Joseph Smith saw Jesus Christ and Heavenly Father, the interaction was part of saving us all. Christ authorized Joseph to speak of that sacred moment. We read in the scriptures of sacred experiences, and they change us.

I feel comfortable sharing some of mine in the hope that they can bring you more joy in Jesus Christ.

The Celestial Room

My first day as a temple ordinance worker, unfortunately, came on a hard day. There had been a great deal of contention in my family that week. People I loved didn't agree with me, and I didn't agree with them. It was frustrating and yet as real as relationships can get. It wasn't the preparation I had hoped for going into my temple service. Regardless, my temple experience, yet again, helped me feel God's promises were real, even though I was getting off track.

As it turned out, during a small part of my shift, I was assigned to watch over the celestial room. But during my designated time, no one was in there.

Miracle #1: I had the celestial room all to myself for a few precious minutes. I reached out to my Heavenly Father in prayer. My mind was jumping between hurt, anger, and confusion. I needed some clarity.

"Heavenly Father, I would really appreciate your perspective on this. How am I supposed to feel? What is the wise thing to do?"

I have learned from experience that as I speak to my Heavenly Father through prayer, He often speaks to me through the scriptures. I picked up one of the Bibles off a table and sat down.

"As I start to read these scriptures, will you give some insight that will help me?" Then I opened the scriptures to a random page and began to read.

Miracle #2: The chapter I opened was Isaiah 60. It is a beautiful, detailed description of the house of Israel (or God's covenant-keeping people) in their royal and glorified state.

"Arise, shine; for thy light is come, and the glory of the Lord is risen upon thee. For, behold, the darkness shall cover the earth, and gross darkness the people: but the Lord shall arise upon thee, and his glory shall be seen upon thee.

"And the Gentiles shall come to thy light, and kings to the brightness of thy rising. Lift up thine eyes round about, and see: all they gather themselves together, they come to thee: thy sons shall come from far, and thy daughters shall be nursed at thy side" (Isaiah 60:1–4).

There is no better place to recognize the reality of this prophecy to the covenant-keeping house of Israel than sitting in the celestial room of one of God's palaces on earth. Is there a better chapter in the whole Bible to remind me that everything is going to turn out just fine? My problem would pass. I was doing the work of glory. My family would come together again. I needed to keep a higher perspective in mind.

Miracle #3: My problem wasn't solved; it just wasn't really a problem anymore. I was motivated to let go of my pride, love more deeply, and talk it out with my family. I had gone to my Father's house as His beloved daughter, and I received the comfort I needed.

We have a great deal of good to get done, and He intends to help us do it through grace, wisdom, and confidence. After I left the celestial room, I was charitable and focused on what my family needed from me. I was also better able to achieve what I wanted most—strong family relationships.

Why did I need to be in the temple to receive this insight? Why didn't I have a better attitude sooner? Because I'm an imperfect human. Perhaps dedicating my time to God in the temple gave me the focus I needed to ask for help. Or maybe it would have been too difficult to internalize "the brightness of [my] rising" anywhere except the celestial room. Regardless of the reason, the fact remains that I have read Isaiah 60 many times, but it never touched my soul or brought tears of joy to my eyes the way it did that day in that sacred space.

The temple is a place of relief, motivation, pure knowledge, and improvement, just the way God intends it to be.

The Initiatory

The idea that I am a queen unto God has sat in my heart and on my mind many times. There are many un-queenly things I do that distract me from this title. One of them is at times making shallow judgments. Many times, I have taken part in the initiatory ordinance, and I have had a nagging thought:

"Why does the space dedicated to our anointing seem so insignificant?"

The tight space and simple decor have felt mismatched to the significant ordinance being performed, especially compared to the other rooms of the temple.

I do not feel this way anymore and have fully repented of my narrow-minded thinking. I had a beautiful experience that testified to me about the reality of our temple promises. It started with me taking a strong interest in Doctrine and Covenants 110. In this section, Joseph Smith recounts his honored visitation with Jesus Christ, Moses, Elijah, and Elias.

Jesus Christ is described in poetic words: "His eyes were as a flame of fire; the hair of his head was white like the pure snow; his countenance shone above the brightness of the sun; and his voice was as the sound of the rushing of great waters" (Doctrine and Covenants 110:3).

He declares Joseph and Oliver Cowdery to be "forgiven" and "clean," and three times speaks of rejoicing. Finally, He prophesies, "Yea the hearts of thousands and tens of thousands shall greatly rejoice in consequence of the blessings which shall be poured out, and the endowment with which my servants have been endowed in this house" (Doctrine and Covenants 110:9).

Immediately thereafter, Moses appears to grant the keys of the gathering of Israel. Then Elias appears to bestow the keys of the

Abrahamic covenant. Elijah appears with the sealing powers. Finally, the moment that took centuries to prepare! Ancient patriarchs with their royal promises could now be linked to us, and we could be linked back to them. Only then could our covenants be new *and* everlasting.

One afternoon of many, I stood in the initiatory area before a worthy and faithful patron. As authorized by priesthood authority, I began to declare the promises linked to these same sacred keys. But this time, a connection occurred to me. When Jesus Christ authorized the use of these keys, He was standing with just two men within a small, unadorned space surrounded by a white curtain.

While the veil did not part for me the way it certainly did for Joseph Smith, perhaps it rustled just a bit. I felt the spirit come over me in a comforting and reassuring way. I imagined Jesus Christ standing so close to me that I thought I could reach out and grab His hand. I felt more with my soul than my eyes saw, but I experienced a closeness to Him like never before. The tightness of the space and simplicity of the room signaled to my mind how little the Lord needs to complete miraculous work.

I testify that the ordinances performed that day were completed with Christ's knowledge and authorization. I knew I was doing the work of the prophets of old in the house of the living God. I hardly deserve such a privilege, but am so humbled to serve my Savior with every ordinance that is completed.

I also felt an impression come to me clearly. We adorn the initiatory. Just as Christ stood upon a work of gold and glowed in full brightness, the woman with me that day brought more than enough beauty into the space. She was spiritually clean and righteously endowed with God's blessing. Never again will I belittle the great designs of God.

The Endowment Room

A few weeks ago, I was assigned as the sister's veil coordinator for my temple shift. In this role, I oversaw several sisters as they supported the sister patrons in completing their endowment sessions.

For some reason, while I waited and watched, some unwelcome thoughts came into my mind. I have a family member who rarely misses the opportunity to say something disparaging about my faith or the Church of Jesus Christ. Her disrespectful words were unwelcome, yet ringing in my ears. I shook my head, wanting to clear them out. Why was I thinking about this at such an inappropriate time?

Meanwhile, patrons had finished the endowment ordinance, and the sister workers supporting them came to me with completed name cards. These name cards record each daughter of God who has just received her endowment. More than her name, the card often relays details of her life: her birthdate, birthplace, or family relations. These cards signify women from various countries, born in various centuries. But each was important and valued by God. Every sister was sought after, served, and wanted.

As each worker passed, these name cards began to stack up in front of me—first five, then ten, then twenty. Finally, as the last card was passed over to me, a clear voice rang in my mind.

"She can have no impact on these women. But you do."

The statement's obvious truthfulness caught me off guard. My hurtful family member does not have the opportunity to support these women, though she may have liked to. She has no power to influence their lives in any way. But I do! Through Jesus Christ, I can reach them across time and space. In a small way, He enlists me to help them achieve what they want the very most. It fills me with gratitude.

I have thought of the lesson I learned that day many times this week. A lone gunman attacked a church house in Michigan, leaving many people traumatized, injured, or killed. The same obvious truth still applies. Even senseless violence cannot stop the work that continues in every temple all over the world. Persecution does not affect whether Jesus Christ will keep His promises to you.

God's children are being endowed with God's power. Work on earth is impacting heaven. Heavenly Father is teaching us the principles of godliness within each temple ordinance (see Doctrine and Covenants 84:17–21).

The Dressing Room

Within the women's dressing room of the Portland Oregon Temple hangs a stunning seascape. This painting is unique. The same painting hangs in three separate locations within the same temple, giving me ample opportunity to view it and ponder it. This painting also hides a hidden meaning.

The artist chose the golden hour of dusk to depict large clouds gathered over sparkling waves, catching the rays of the setting sun. Just inches over the horizon, the sun burns warmly in a soft yellow, tinging the clouds in heavenly tones of pink, apricot, and amber. Up front, the waves crest onto the beach and spread across the sand. Having experienced the Oregon coastline on many evenings such as this, the scene takes on a look of perfection, yet it is wonderfully realistic.

One could walk past this painting, appreciate the beauty of the landscape, and pass by, being fully satisfied with the peace it offers. The first time I saw the piece, I noticed three sweet cloud figures just off-center to the left. They almost looked like three little cloud-people seated in a row with the perfect view of the setting sun. I had not yet caught the deeper message.

Expertly camouflaged, leering at these little figures, hides a wolf in sheep's clothing. His dark gray face peeks out from the largest cloud structure of pinks and creams. His gray arm stretches to the side, as if to instruct those little clouds to move away from their view of the sun and off the canvas.

This painting clearly depicts Satan's influence over each of us. It was disheartening to see that the wolf marred the sanctity of the temple. Still, the picture held more meaning. A few more weeks of pondering this scene, and I saw the hope it is meant to convey. From the top of the wolf's head, long, thin wisps are dissipating into the clear sky. The warmth of the sun is evaporating the wolf away! The golden sun is indeed still shining on the faces of those little people. The golden light rolls forward, caught in the endless stream of waves as they break onto the shore. No cloud, even with a hidden wolf, can hinder them now. The sun is very close to dropping into twilight, just as our Savior is very close to rising with the dawn of His Second Coming.

The Masterclass of Jesus Christ

The world can feel like a troubled place, marked by unpredictable outcomes and chaotic forces. Do not be afraid of the world in which your Savior has placed you. He has a plan in place to help you overcome as He did, walk on water as Peter did, and receive power as Joseph Smith did. The temple endowment will enable you to gain the power of Jesus Christ. It is a key part of the comfort, safety, and hope offered by your Heavenly Father.

From Adam and Eve to the testimonies of the earliest Latter-day Saints, the scriptures have given us examples of ordinary people overpowering, outsmarting, and maneuvering around Satan. The principles of obedience, sacrifice, doctrine, chastity, and consecration have always been the tools they used. They have always worked successfully!

The temple endowment can teach you the same principles until you understand them and trust them enough to integrate them into your character. In this way, you can take on the attributes of Jesus Christ. In this way, Jesus Christ can share His power with you.

God's Miracles

Miracles are a gift to the many, not just one, so the ripple effects can spread far and wide. When Joseph Smith saw Jesus Christ and Heavenly Father, the interaction could not have been more sacred or personal. Yet the experience was meant for us all to know it and love it. We read in the scriptures of deeply sacred experiences. They change us and inspire our faithful actions.

Sometimes my seminary students express a disappointment that similar miracles are not happening in our day. They want to witness angels and even Goliaths. They want to watch the parting of the Red Sea and know they are part of God's work. After reading a full book on the promise of God's power through covenant-keeping, does a part of you feel the same? I wonder if perception is part of the problem. Perhaps we are not accurately acknowledging the miracles within our daily lives. Perhaps we are glossing them over as common, coincidence, or insignificant. Perhaps we don't fully recognize their scope.

For example, when my father was a small child, he and his younger brother were saved from drowning by a spiritual prompting that came to my grandfather a far distance away. It was a miracle they were saved, and everyone rejoiced in it. But was it a miracle just for that afternoon? Were the benefits meant just for my father and his brother? No. For me, it was as if I was pulled from the water that day. The miracle altered my life that day as much as it did my father's. You have probably never met my father (you'd remember if you had), but since you are reading his daughter's book, the saving of his life also played a part in this very moment of your life. My point being that we are impacted by more of God's coordination than we can possibly know.

When I shared the story of quitting my job in New York, that miracle was not meant to impact only my first child, but especially my second and my third and their children that will come after.

I have highlighted many ancient prophets within this book. Were their miracles meant to affect just them? Were their miraculous outcomes just for their benefit? No. Every step they took brought us all a step closer to God's ultimate goal of sharing His power with us. The miracles of our days are built upon the miracles of their days. Their miracles are linked to us just as Abraham's covenants are linked to us. All collective miracles will culminate in God's greatest miracle: us becoming like Him.

In ancient times, Peter escaped Herod's prison with the help of an angel. But temple work today is opening the gates to a far larger spirit prison in heaven. Which is the greater miracle? The covenant-keepers who have escaped this spirit prison far outnumber the Israelites that escaped Pharoh by crossing the Red Sea on dry land. Which is the greater miracle? These escaped children of the covenant represent an army of Davids who have conquered their Goliath. Which is the greater miracle? Esther was chosen and anointed as queen so she could save her people. But through the Restoration millions of kings and queens of the House of Israel have been chosen and anointed within God's temples. Which miracle will save more souls? Which miracle represents more of God's power?

My testimony to you is the temple of God is a source of His power manifest in our day for the benefit of all His children. Your work in the temple will have a positive impact on even those you love who do not yet choose to enter the temple. We can use this opportunity to take part in miracles greater than God has yet performed!

Acknowledgments

Fretting is not something I typically did before I started working on this manuscript. Fretting has now developed into a long-term condition over the last five years. I have started and stopped this writing process on multiple occasions because it has been difficult for me to embrace the task the Spirit has directed, often with a fair amount of trepidation. As the first ideas filtered forward, they honestly scared me. Better to file those ideas away in the deep pockets of my mind rather than assume I could write on the sacred experience of God's endowment. I was still new to a detailed word-by-word working relationship with the great Master Editor. The full picture of what He intended me to do had not fully materialized in my mind.

The first step was to edit my perspective, then my nerves. I had to embrace the idea that the soul-churning process of my first book was only just the beginning. Next, I had to convince my husband that, regardless of what else needed to get done, I could not get the prompting to write out of my mind.

Many days were spent struggling with inspiration, knowing I could not move on until the correct answer and tone were found. Many late nights, I was unable to sleep until the flood of inspiration was written down. Many early mornings were spent being jolted straight off my pillow as a new thought reoriented a whole chapter. At one point, which now feels like a long time ago, I felt at peace with the manuscript. It felt like I had done what I set out to do, and I breathed a deep breath of satisfaction. It was short-lived. A week later, blissfully unaware while working in the initiatory area of the temple, even in mid-sentence, a download of edits crowded out my mind, making me lose my train of thought. The book is now thirty pages longer than it once was.

In short, the writing process was difficult. The most accurate acknowledgment to be given is to admit that I have been difficult for the Holy Ghost to work with. I should have been more diligent; I should have trusted with less trepidation. I should have allowed fewer distractions. The process has also been one of the most spiritually fortifying of my life. There is great safety as the Master Editor holds your hand. Seeing this pattern repeated in my life, not just in my writing, has made me feel less vulnerable and less exposed than I once did. This book will forever be a treasured physical reminder of the progress that can be accomplished day by day under the direction of the Holy Ghost and the grace of Jesus Christ. This work is imperfect in every way, but it has also been made better every day by my Savior. The strength of His conviction to uphold these comprehensive promises is astounding.

My handsome, patient, glorious husband has endured many rewrites, many less productive days waiting for answers to come, many pouty days of frustration. He has also never faltered in his support and encouragement. Who is better suited than my own husband to say, "You don't know what you're talking about!" But instead, he is almost more eager for this book to be published than I am. Bless his heart!

I have had several beta readers review early editions, providing their insights to help shape the final product. Athena Lau and Elijah Pierce were wonderfully helpful with their particular detail. Each beta reader has offered various and unique inputs from different spiritual backgrounds, attention spans, ages, and temple experience. I included a broad range of individuals who can relate to this book through its writing style. It is the work of the beta readers who have removed obstacles that may have hindered many others.

To my daughters, Ashley and Evie, thank you for your honest assessments and sincere investments in this project. To my daughter Natalie, your words and perspective have been on my mind constantly.

When God gives us a task to complete, it is rarely just about the individual; He intends the work to involve many others nearby. If there is any reason why God asked me to write on this topic, it may have more to do with my family than me individually.

Thank you to the team at Cedar Fort Publishing and Media for taking on this work. My initial editor, Liz Kazandzhy, caught the vision of what I intended and helped refine the rough edges into a clearer picture that more people can enjoy. She was willing to consider a new perspective while offering the guidance and experience I lacked. Her work is wonderfully appreciated.

Jessica Lawrence, also of Cedar Fort, was my own personal Hermione Granger. Bless her for the dedication and time she put into making this work as beneficial to readers as possible. Her detailed thought processes uncovered better opportunities to teach important ideas and polished away unnecessary distractions. The final product was greatly improved through her insights.

Notes

1. Russell M. Nelson, *Let God Prevail,* General Conference (Salt Lake City: The Church of Jesus Christ of Latter-day Saints), Oct. 2020, Gospel Library App.
2. Modern revelation has not specified the identity of this divine wrestler. I have portrayed this story literally between Jacob and God the Father to illustrate the battle we all fight between our faith and our fears. Consider also that Jacob wrestled *and* was given a covenant with a covenantal name. Today, such covenants are made with God the Father in temples. Just as Enos "wrestled" all night in prayer to God the Father, here Jacob testifies he saw God "face-to-face." I love this story because it shows evidence of God the Father as a resurrected Man. He understands the impulses of His human children on a deep level. Further commentary can be found from Andrew C. Skinner, former dean of Religious Education at Brigham Young University. (See Andrew C. Skinner, "Jacob in the Presence of God," in *Sperry Symposium Classics: The Old Testament*, ed. Paul Y. Hoskisson [Religious Studies Center, Brigham Young University, and Deseret Book, 2005], 117–132.)
3. See also Bradley R. Wilcox, *O Youth of the Noble Birthright,* General Conference (Salt Lake City: The Church of Jesus Christ of Latter-day Saints), Oct. 2024, Gospel Library App.
4. Russell M. Nelson, *Drawing the Power of Jesus Christ into Our Lives,* General Conference (Salt Lake City: The Church of Jesus Christ of Latter-day Saints), Apr. 2017, Gospel Library App.
5. Russell M. Nelson, "Creation," *Ensign*, May 2000, 84; Mark E. Petersen, "Adam, the Archangel," *Ensign*, Nov. 1980, 16.
6. Bible Dictionary, "War in Heaven"; see also Doctrine and Covenants 76:19–38.
7. Russell M. Nelson, "Choices for Eternity" [worldwide devotional for young adults, May 15, 2022], Gospel Library.

8. Jeffery R Holland, *And Now I See*, General Conference (Salt Lake City: The Church of Jesus Christ of Latter-day Saints), Oct. 2025, Gospel Library App.
9. M. Russell Ballard, The Law of Sacrifice, Church Education System, Brigham Young University Aug. 13, 1996, Gospel Library App.
10. Further context has been taught by Elder James E. Talmage (*Jesus the Christ* [1916], 43). See also Romans 16:20; Hebrews 2:14.
11. Russell M. Nelson, *We Can Do Better and Be Better*, General Conference (Salt Lake City: The Church of Jesus Christ of Latter-day Saints), Apr. 2019, Gospel Library App.
12. More insight is offered in "The Father and the Son: A Doctrinal Exposition by the First Presidency and the Quorum of the Twelve Apostles," reprinted in *Ensign*, April 2002. Also see Russell M. Nelson, "Think Celestial!" *Liahona*, November 2023.
13. For further reading on these deeply sacred topics search out divinely appointed sources such as the words of prophets and apostles. Godly ambitions and expectations are beyond our current understanding because we do not yet see the full picture of exaltation. They can be easily misunderstood or taken out of proper context. A reliable source of study would be the Gospel Topic Essays found in the Gospel Library App. May I recommend the essay entitled "Becoming Like God."
14. Bradley R. Wilcox, *O Youth of the Noble Birthright*, General Conference (Salt Lake City: The Church of Jesus Christ of Latter-day Saints), Oct. 2024, Gospel Library App.
15. Russell M. Nelson and Wendy W. Nelson, "Hope of Israel" (worldwide youth devotional, June 3, 2018), Gospel Library.

About the Author

Sharla Goettl was raised soaking up the Arizona sunshine but now resides under the lush trees of Oregon with her capable husband and three young adult daughters. Sharla and Chris Goettl own and operate a residential construction business. She earned a degree in business management and leadership.

Sharla has mentored the youth in various church callings for over twenty years, such as stake Young Women president and seminary teacher. Currently, her happy place is the Portland Oregon Temple where she serves as an ordinance worker. In 2021, Sharla published her debut book, *Spiritual Resilience: Leading Our Youth to Go and Do.* Whether speaking at conferences or teaching early in the morning, Sharla is privileged to share the good news of Jesus Christ.

Connect with Sharla, keep up with her next project, or read some of her short stories at www.sharlagoettl.com or on Instagram @authorsharlagoettl.

Scan to visit

https://sharlagoettl.com/